D0829975

# TRANSFORMING THE
# CLUNKY ORGANIZATION

THE *PRAGMATIC LEADERSHIP* SERIES

# TRANSFORMING THE CLUNKY ORGANIZATION

## Pragmatic Leadership Skills for Breaking Inertia

SAMUEL B. BACHARACH

Published in Association with Cornell University Press

ITHACA AND LONDON

Copyright © 2018 by Samuel B. Bacharach

All rights reserved. Except for brief quotations in a review, this book, or parts thereof, must not be reproduced in any form without permission in writing from the publisher. For information, address Cornell University Press, Sage House, 512 East State Street, Ithaca, New York 14850. Visit our website at cornellpress.cornell.edu.

First published 2018 by Cornell University Press

Printed in the United States of America

Design by Scott Levine

Library of Congress Cataloging-in-Publication Data

Names: Bacharach, Samuel B., author.
Title: Transforming the clunky organization : pragmatic leadership skills for breaking inertia / Samuel B. Bacharach.
Description: Ithaca [New York] : Cornell University Press, 2018. | Series: The pragmatic leadership series | Includes bibliographical references.
Identifiers: LCCN 2018006070 (print) | LCCN 2018007687 (ebook) | ISBN 9781501710056 (epub/mobi) | ISBN 9781501710049 (pdf) | ISBN 9781501710599| ISBN 9781501710599 (cloth : alk. paper) | ISBN 9781501710032 (pbk. : alk. paper)
Subjects: LCSH: Organizational change. | Organizational effectiveness. | Leadership. | Executive ability. | Organizational behavior.
Classification: LCC HD58.8 (ebook) | LCC HD58.8 .B335 2018 (print) | DDC 658.4/092--dc23
LC record available at https://lccn.loc.gov/2018006070

To my ILR students who have
accompanied me on this journey. Thank you!
(1974–2016)

# Contents

# Preface

## THE PRAGMATIC LEADER AND ORGANIZATIONAL INERTIA

Organizational leadership is not an end. It's a pragmatic means to solve a problem!

To appreciate why organizational leadership is important, there needs to be a recognition of the core problems that organizational leaders try to solve. The premise of this book is that the primary organizational challenge for leaders is overcoming inertia.

Have you ever noticed that many organizations are "doing fine" but just miss the mark? While there is a sense that they are doing fine—and sometimes very fine—they do not quite reach their potential. They are not as agile as they'd like to be, not as responsive to the markets as they used to be, new ideas are no longer incorporated easily, opportunities fall between the cracks, and execution is a bit clumsy. They aren't going to go out of business tomorrow, but they are showing symptoms of inertia. Indeed, these organizations are not necessarily failing or even on the brink of failure. Some the greatest and best-known organizations go through periods of sluggishness. What makes them vulnerable to inertia? How can inertia be avoided? *Pragmatic leaders have the skills to break inertia.*

There are two sources of organizational inertia: the clunky tendency and the myopic tendency. The clunky tendency emerges when the organization has unintegrated structures, diffuse authority, overlapping goals, and a general sense of organized anarchy. The myopic tendency is reinforced by outdated practices and old business models. The challenge for pragmatic leaders is to overcome these sources of inertia to make sure that their organizations thrive and reach their potential. They overcome the inertia perpetuated by either clunky or myopic tendencies by making sure that their organizations engage in discovery and delivery.

To break inertia, pragmatic leaders engage in robust discovery by constantly reading the environment, picking up new ideas, and translating those ideas into concrete innovations, changes, and agendas. They then focus on delivery, making sure that these new ideas gain support in their organization, are implemented, and become an integral part of the organization's agenda rather than fall into the abyss of unfulfilled aspiration.

Using examples drawn from various organizations, leaders, and contexts, section 1 examines the sources of inertia and the organizational challenges inertia presents. Sections 2 and 3 introduce the specific, executable skills pragmatic leaders need to break inertia: *robust discovery* and *focused delivery*. Section 2 specifically delves into robust discovery, examining the pragmatic leadership capacity to explore and ideate. Pragmatic leaders need to be *contextually competent* and explore their environment to understand external challenges and opportunities. They also must be *ideationally competent* to make sure that ideas gain traction and result in concrete innovation. Section 3 examines the facets of focused delivery, the pragmatic leadership capacity to be *politically competent* to gain support for ideas, innovations, and projects while being *managerially competent*, capable of sustaining positive momentum to make sure the ball is not dropped.

If the core challenge of leadership is to make sure that organizations do not become sluggish but thrive and reach their potential, then the simple leadership clichés of inspiration, charisma, great ideas, and interpersonal charm will not suffice. Nor is it enough to talk about "execution" in the abstract. To break inertia, leaders must concern themselves with pragmatic action directed at five core questions:

- Why is the organization sluggish?
- What's out there?
- What can be done about it?
- What support is needed?
- How to implement?

This volume is predicated on the assumption that leaders who have the capacity, not simply to ask these questions, but to do something about the challenges embedded in them, will assure discovery and delivery, thus moving their organization ahead.

# Acknowledgments

At any stage in one's career, writing a book is an accomplishment. But at this later point in my career, I very well know that while accomplishments should be recognized, it is the journey that should be celebrated. There is an old expression in Yiddish that life depends more on luck than on brains. Certainly, that is true of my academic career. Two people made my academic career possible. First, Koya Azumi, who as a young instructor at New York University, on his way to the University of Wisconsin, suggested that I may want to follow his trek out west and consider doing my PhD there. And then there is Michael Aiken, who in 1972 took a chance on a first-generation college graduate from Brooklyn and invited me to join him in Belgium to study the structure of local governments. With that gesture, and with his tutoring through my dissertation, Michael single-handedly opened up a door to a forty-year career. These two are the pillars on which everything else rests.

Ed Lawler, my friend for almost fifty years. Along the way we wrote some books and articles. But who cares? What is important is that for fifty years we have spoken at least twice a week. David Lipsky, who befriended me and guided my early years at Cornell University, and tends to give me more credit than I deserve. Bill Sonnenstuhl, a continuous presence in my family's life, and an uncle to my son. And the ever-present Peter Bamberger, with whom I've shared many a project.

While Peter was my premier graduate student and has well exceeded my academic record—and in that, I take great pride—what I truly take great pride in is that the Bacharach and Bamberger families are so enmeshed in friendship.

My Cornell University career has been enriched by an amazing cohort. To name a few: Nick Salvatore, the consummate Brooklyn truck driver, a great historian, has always served as an academic role model. Esta Bigler, a person with whom on any day I could have a real-world conversation, has been an upward mobility partner. Harry Katz, a low-key leader, has modeled for many of us what authentic leadership is about. Bob Smith, the reasonable yet deeply giving associate dean who kept the ILR School going, is proof that leadership is indeed about execution. Tove Hammer and I came to Cornell together as very, very young people. She with her sports car, and I with my attitude. Over the years I appreciated more and more her values, her commitment, and her sense of continuity.

You never write a book alone. I would like to acknowledge the many undergraduates who have shared ideas with me over the years. From my introductory 120 courses in my early years to my weekly internship class in New York City, ILR undergraduates have taught me much.

I am also grateful to the unique graduate students who were part of the New York City–based Master of Professional Studies program, which I was involved with since its inception. These were the best of adult learners, who freely shared their experience and their ideas. Sara Edwards made my life easier by sustaining this program, a remarkable accomplishment.

Just as my students have been of great assistance, I have learned much from a cadre of practitioners from such organizations as Cisco and SunGard. In particular, I would like to mention Jonathan Rosenberg of the collaborative technology group at Cisco, with whom I had two critical conversations that impacted some of the key concepts of this volume. Brian Hull of UBS was also an important early read-er of the manuscript, who shared many insights about leadership. Kathleen Weslock, executive vice president and chief people officer at Frontier Communications,  has been supremely supportive of my efforts to bridge academia with the real world. My close colleague Gi-anpaolo Barozzi spent many hours in discussion with me in Milan, New York City, and around the world, sharing his unique insights and friendship. Rob Rothman grasped the essence of this book early and understood the importance of the transformation of the clunky organization, suggesting the initial title. Andy Doyle, executive vice president and chief human resources officer at OppenheimerFunds, is a superb academic and practitioner partner who allows me to steal his toast at our monthly omelet breakfasts at the diner on Fourteenth Street. Ken DiPietro took the time and the patience to thoroughly read the manuscript and make important critiques, for which I am immensely grateful.

Johnson Jose of Cisco, Sara Sepehr of FIS Global, Oliver Muhr of Seerene, and Joseph Drago have been incredibly supportive of my ef-forts. Chris Proulx has been a tremendous colleague for more than ten years. He is a person who hung in there with me and continuously served as an amazing sounding board. I would also like to thank Dan Silvershein, one of the most remarkable critics and readers it has been my good fortune to have on my side.

Paul Salvatore, with whom I had numerous discussions about lead-ers and with whom I occasionally cotaught, has always been avail-able. The quiet, occasional lunches with Doug Braunstein, whom I've known since he was an undergraduate, give me a sense of continuity. Rob Manfred, who gives me too much credit, has been a source of affirmation. Winston Feng, the youngest of the lot, is a perpetual re-invigorating force. Fran Bonsignore has been a mentor and a guide. Marty Schmelkin continuously brings me back to roots.

When I was struggling with a core theme, Kaushik Basu brought his light touch to the subject and led me to focus on inertia. Kimberly Weisul, a talented writer, is a person who understands the state of contemporary organizations. She, too, was a sounding board at numerous stages along the way. I also thank my collegues at *Inc.* magazine who gave me an outlet for my academic and nonacademic ideas: Eric Shurenberg, Laura Lorber, and Janice Lombardo.

The initial support I received from James Briggs, who saw the importance and value of writing an integrative leadership volume, was critical. His patience and persistence were crucial at a difficult start for these ideas. Ariel Avgar, my newest colleague at Cornell, has been a wonderful critic and a delightful addition to my journey. Jack Goncalo, with his often very clever insights and sharp humor, keeps on giving me good ideas and helps me keep things in context. The political wit and quick insights of Dan McCray have always kept me on my toes for the last number of years. My friend and colleague Joe Grasso, the man with the eye for detail, has taught me the importance of making sure that everything is approved by the watchdogs. And Kevin Hallock, the next generation of academic leaders, is a person who will have to deal with the challenges I write about, and has the capacity to do so.

There are three Cornell University leaders from whom I've learned a great deal and who have been superb partners: Mary Opperman, vice president of human resources, is the superb master of people skills, organizational processes, and organizational values. Elmira Mangum, who was vice president for planning and budget, understands how to balance politics and reality. Ted Dodds, who was vice president for information technologies and chief information officer, taught me much about how difficult it is to move good ideas in the world of turf and tradition. All three are masters at surviving in a clunky organization.

In the last fifteen years I've delved into the world of training. And there I had some major mentors and partners, people who taught me how to get my message across. Dana Vashdi, Yael Bacharach, Kathryn Burkgren, and Chris Halladay have taught me the art of taking my time, listening to others, shutting my mouth, and putting participants first.

I appreciate my colleagues at Cornell University Press. My books are a new venture for them and it took a courageous editor, Dean Smith, head of Cornell University Press, to take a chance on moving into a new market. I appreciate his partnership. Martyn Beeny, whom I've often frustrated, continues to support and push these efforts. Ange Romeo-Hall, whose editorial talents tolerated my ramblings. And Scott Levine, the minimalist artist, with a wonderful, light touch. Fran Benson, one of the great developmental editors, whose career is reflected in the masterful work she's produced. Having Fran believe in my capacity is more than gratifying.

When the rubber hit the road, I had the good fortune of working with a remarkable group of research assistants, who have subsequently become colleagues and friends. Saaylee Potnis came to this project at such a critical point that I cannot thank her enough for her initial support and detailed work. Through her, I met Neha Arun Joshi and Megha Saraf, who built on Saaylee's insights and allowed me to delve into better examples. Peter Baek came in at the late stages of this work, but researched some of the most difficult examples and really got me through a lurch. Thank you to the very bright Trevor Smith, who was the best undergraduate editor I ever worked with, and for the focus of Meher Kanigiri. Each of these individuals gave generously of their time, intellect, and perspiration. I am deeply, deeply grateful to them.

As with any project, it comes down to the core team. Napoleon Zapata, whom I met during his junior year at Cornell University, not only interned with me but also completed his master's degree with me. I take great pride in our accomplishments and in our friendship. He has been a superior critic, a thorough researcher, and a truly supportive young friend. At moments when I was most disillusioned, he saw the light at the end of the tunnel. If any person served as a key researcher on this volume, it's Napoleon. His thoroughness, his diligence, his talent have enriched these efforts.

One of the high points of my career is working with Katie Briggs. She has been coordinator of a number of major grants, the manager of the Smithers Institute, and the best critic and academic editor I know. The sixteen years we've worked together, at least for me, have been a remarkable joy. None of my career accomplishments during this period would have occurred without her. Sometimes we see things differently, and see the world wearing different glasses, and indeed, we have different backgrounds. But as in any working relationship, its strength comes from sharing common core values. My gratitude to her as a colleague and a friend for her generosity is unbounded.

Finally, I would like to thank my wife, Yael Bacharach, who continues to give me perspective and constantly reminds me that our cup is more than half full. Then there is my son, Ben, who this year will graduate from Cornell University, and who has been and will be the presence that helps me define what is human.

Thank you all.

# TRANSFORMING THE CLUNKY ORGANIZATION

# 1

# THE CHALLENGE OF INERTIA

## SLUGGISH ORGANIZATIONS: CLUNKY AND MYOPIC

Organizations, like people, sometimes get stuck. They get ensnared in routines and processes, and they fall back into old habits. Sometimes fatigue dominates, complexity overwhelms, and organizational energy is drained. In these instances, the capacity to innovate, move agendas, and push things forward is constrained by the security of routine and the comfort of the mundane. Leaders become risk averse, repeating what was successful yesterday or last year as the safest course of action. They have trouble recapturing the same zest, agility, and dynamic energy that were essential in the past. They become sluggish—they get trapped by inertia. Business theorist Jeffrey Pfeffer defines inertia as "an inability for an organization to change as rapidly as the environment."[1] Inertia connotes a certain sense of comfort with the familiar and a reticence to go beyond the tried and true.

The real danger zone for organizations is the stage that precedes failure—that is, the period of inertia, the period in which the organization begins to show signs of sluggishness. They aren't able to engage in discovery and delivery as agilely as they had in the past. If organizations do not deal with the challenges of inertia, they risk fading away.

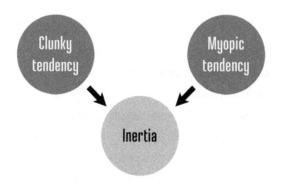

Structural clunkiness and the myopic mind-set are the two fundamental sources of organizational inertia and sluggishness. The clunky tendency is not a state of chaos but a state of organized anarchy. On the surface, there is a veneer of order, but underneath are overlapping structures, unclear decision processes, chaotic communication, and poor integration. The myopic tendency emerges when organizations are overly focused and consumed by their past successes and past behaviors. When the myopic tendency dominates, decision making is shaped by the blinder mind-set, and organizations find it difficult to adjust their goals or revisit their business model even though circumstances demand it. To break inertia, pragmatic leaders need to understand the sources of clunky and myopic tendencies.

## The Inertia of the Clunky Tendency

When an organization tends toward clunkiness, it is often in a state of organized anarchy. Organized calls to mind a succinctly integrated, systematically efficient social order, while anarchy conjures up images of disordered chaos, sprawl, and turmoil. Looked at from the outside, organizations with clunky tendencies appear to be organized. When they are looked at from the inside out, however, or when someone tries to make sense of how to move agendas within the organization, their anarchistic qualities become apparent. That is, they are chaotic and have an element of sprawl. All the components are there, and the organization trucks along, but it is not clear how the organization functions.

In an organized anarchy, individual units, departments, or businesses may be successful. However, in the aggregate, the organization may be less than the sum of its parts. The businesses may not be integrated, accountability may be diffuse, turf and silos may dominate, goal confusion may be common, competing agendas may be in play, and different departments may pull the organization in different directions.

Clunky organizations may have a mission statement and a strategic vision, but when it comes to interpreting the mission statement or vision, there may be anarchy when units and subunits try to impose their specific agenda on the organizational intent. That is, the organization's mission and strategic vision are subject to the intentions of individual units that may reframe the organizational goals to rationalize the unit's specific course of action. This loose alignment of organizational and unit goals feeds the sense of clunkiness.

In the context of unclear alignment between organizational and unit goals, units and individuals may create their own procedures and processes as they see fit, losing operational consistency. In this context, actions define procedure rather than the other way around. Muddling through becomes the art of the day. That is, "participants arrive at an interpretation of what they are doing and what they have done while in the process of doing it."[2] In fact, from business to business, project to project, and unit to unit, authority constantly shifts, and the role of subtle interpersonal influence processes should not be underestimated. Essentially, the journey is defined as the organizational actor proceeds, one step at a time. In a clunky organization, muddling through is a survival tactic.[3]

Progress in an organization with clunky tendencies requires tremendous effort, continuous deliberation, and exhausting coordination. It can demand the energy of Sisyphus, who was tasked for eternity to push a stone uphill only to have it roll back before he could reach the top. But clunkiness does not necessarily doom an organization. Clunky organizations are disproportionally large, resource rich, and conventionally successful, but at the same time they are unwieldy and clumsily plod from project to project. That is, they are not necessarily failing, but they are not exactly thriving either. They are sluggish, and are unable to meet their potential because of their clunkiness.

The clunky tendency can make an organization sluggish because the flow of information may not be smooth and continuous, the allocation of resources is diffuse, responsibilities are duplicated, and efforts at developing and sustaining customer relationships, marketing and sales, and innovation are often uncoordinated. Clunky organizations are networked in such a disjointed way that they develop what sociologist Ronald Burt calls "structural holes"[4]—that is, gaps in information sharing across an organization. There are gaps between organizational units that possess complementary information and conduct corresponding activities. Burt observes, "The structural hole between two groups does not mean that people in the groups are unaware of one another. It only means that the people are focused on their own activities such that they do not attend to the activities of people in the other group. Holes are buffers, like an insulator in an electric circuit. People on either side of a structural hole circulate in different flows of information."[5]

The combination of these elements results in an organization that never quite gets its act together. The organization never establishes a sense of continuous focus, leading to duplication and inefficiencies.

Before its 2011 restructuring, Cisco was a sluggish organization exhibiting clunky tendencies. Cisco's structure was byzantine, sprawling, and bureaucratic. It was a classic organized anarchy operating as a clunky organization. The decision-making process was steered by "59 internal standing committees."[6] It was the norm for top executives to serve on ten or more committees and spend almost a third of their time dealing with committee work.[7] This decision-making process enhanced Cisco's clunky tendencies, making operations much more cumbersome. Brian White, an analyst with Ticonderoga Securities, observed at the time, "People at Cisco are constantly going to meetings. . . . I just wonder if everyone has the time to innovate as much as they would like or as much as the company would like."[8]

In late 2007, rival HP upgraded the warranty for its switches to include free upgrades and support.[9] Under Cisco's then-clunky structure, a decision about how to respond to HP's challenge was delayed as it worked its way through multiple committees. By the time a response to match HP's promotion made it through the unwieldy bureaucracy in April 2009, Cisco's market share had already fallen.

Unilever, the Anglo-Dutch consumer products company, has a global reach, and is another example of an obviously successful organization that has clunky tendencies. Its lack of integration, lack of consensus, and enormous catalog of brands—popular household items that stock cupboards from the Americas to Europe to the Near and Far East—make tight operational integration nearly impossible. The diversity of its product offerings makes even superficial collaboration difficult. For instance, what do Axe body spray and Ben & Jerry's ice cream have in common?

The clunky tendencies of large multinational conglomerates like Unilever are not necessarily a result of their exhaustive catalog of products, but are due to the complexities that arise from internal structures and processes. By 2009, Unilever had over four hundred intranets, one for each country, product, group, brand, and function.[10] While the cost of maintaining multiple sites was expensive, the complexity was not just hampering the financials. The silos were resulting in dysfunctional communication, and employees were unsure where to look for information. Not being able to access the right information quickly affects employee response time. Every country Unilever operates in has very different HR processes, which results in incomplete or inconsistent data records and consequently impedes its ability to manage talent effectively.

Unilever has undoubtedly been successful in establishing its global presence and offering a wide range of products. However, mounting internal complexity slowed processes and information flow. Unilever's lack of integration, lack of consensus, and its size resulted in some inevitable clunkiness. Unilever's clunkiness does not necessarily result in it being stuck, but there is no question that some degree of sluggishness and inertia occurs.

To understand why some organizations experience periods of clunkiness, it helps to trace their growth pattern. Incremental organic growth takes place when organizations can attract new customers, expand output, or increase sales, usually in a measured or incremental manner. When growth is planned, incremental, evaluated, and monitored, it is unlikely that the organization will develop clunky tendencies. Sprawling inorganic growth usually occurs when the ambitions of the organization or the demands of the market become the primary motivating apparatus.

Sprawling expansion that is likely to result in clunkiness occurs when an organization continuously expands its internal capacity without a thorough and thoughtful consideration of what the expansion means or it becomes an unthinking and voracious consumer of other firms. In either case, the organization is in danger of becoming clunky and losing not only its agility but also its reputation for innovation and creativity.

**Sprawling Expansion**

Starbucks experienced an episode of sprawling expansion. The company was founded in 1971 not as a coffee shop but as a place to sell coffee beans and coffee-making equipment. In 1982, Howard Schultz joined the company as head of retail operations and marketing. A year later, he traveled to Italy, and was greatly impressed by the Italian coffee culture. From this moment, the trajectory of Starbucks changed from being a retail outlet for coffee beans to becoming a purveyor of coffee drinks, with the first caffe latte served in 1984.[11] While CEO from 1987–2000, Schultz inaugurated a period of aggressive growth and increased the number of Starbucks locations from seventeen to over 3,500. It wasn't to last. By 2007 there were indications that the company had grown too fast, too quickly, and was becoming clunky. Individual stores did not share a cohesive, integrated feel. Too many ambitious innovations and a slew of new products overwhelmed customers, undermining the intimate coffee shop environment. This clunky tendency and lack of integration did not in any way inhibit growth. Indeed, it was a consequence of growth. Starbucks scaled up, but at the cost of losing its ability to sustain brand value. Without a thoughtful, guiding hand present in organic growth, the wild nature of inorganic growth led to a dilution of the core mission, killing the customer experience. Profits stagnated, and the stock price took a hit. Starbucks felt the brutal consequences of improperly managed growth.

Sprawling expansion resulted in the loss of a coherent mission. Individual stores competed against each other in areas with a Starbucks on every corner, where a store manager's efforts to build customer loyalty would be discounted as new stores appeared. Unfocused innovations and upscaling turned off old and new customers alike, driving consumers away and damaging their base. As John Quelch noted, "None of this need have happened if Starbucks had stayed private and grown at a more controlled pace."[12] In other words, Starbucks became clunky.

If the Starbucks story was a movie, then this is the point where Schultz would swoop back in as CEO and save the day. And in 2008, that is exactly what happened. The Starbucks brand was defined by the quality of coffee and the customer experience, and Schultz directed multiple efforts to reemphasize these factors. He "temporarily closed 7,100 US stores to retrain baristas on how to make the perfect espresso."[13] He decided that Starbucks would only deliver whole-bean coffee to the stores so baristas would grind fresh coffee for the customers.[14] He cleared out the media entertainment products that cluttered the stores.[15] He had the stores redesigned to "recapture the coffeehouse feel"[16] with improved lighting and in-store furnishings. Schultz succeeded in getting Starbucks back on track: "Over the next two years he led Starbucks' massive turnaround, with profits tripling from $315 million to $945 million by 2010."[17] Schultz, the man who had originally put Starbucks on the path to sprawling expansion, was the leader who turned the company around by confronting its clunky tendencies and reinstating a focused, central mission.

Sprawling expansion, as experienced by Starbucks, is growth for its own sake. Starbucks was driven to grow exponentially but temporarily lost sight of those elements that sustained the organization as an integrated whole. Such unsupported inorganic growth can lead to clunkiness and an inability to thrive.

Dell Inc. is an example of an organization that grew inorganically through sprawling expansion. Once a dominant force in the computer industry, Dell became a clunky giant and was forced to go private. Before the exit to private, Dell was arguably a large, resource-rich organization with multiple goals. It was clunky, which was a far cry from its origins in a dorm room at the University of Texas–Austin. The model for selling personal computers on the nascent consumer market was akin to selling cars. Customers had to visit a store or showroom to make a purchase. Michael Dell's innovation was to sell computers (that he designed and built) directly to customers. Customers loved the model of buying computers directly from the manufacturer, and as prices were driven down, sales escalated, reaching a peak in 2005. That year the company topped *Fortune's* list of "America's Most Admired Companies."[18]

The conventional wisdom was that Dell needed to diversify even more to hold their ground. Dell complied by creating different product lines for different customers, from the Vostro to the Dell Latitude series of PCs. Dell was growing, but growing in the wrong ways. It was becoming clunky. In 2007, in a frank interview with Spiegel Online, Michael Dell noted that "head count grew by 50 percent to about 80,000 employees while revenues grew by just 15 percent. That's not a good idea."[19] When asked what these people were doing, Dell responded: "We've been asking ourselves that same question. I think the organization got too complicated. We made it too complicated. The CEO had too many people reporting to him, each person reporting to the CEO had an organization to support him, and then these had their own supporting organizations and so on. It multiplied out to be a whole lot of people. Everyone was well-intentioned, everyone went to work saying 'We're going to do great work today,' but when you add it all up, the structure didn't work out."[20]

Even though Dell realized that there were problems and tried to fix them, the clunky nature of the organization made turnaround difficult. Dell made more than a dozen acquisitions between 2010 and 2012—some in new areas, like security, making integration more difficult. Financial losses continued to dog the firm into 2013, when the chairman, Michael Dell, successfully orchestrated a plan to take the company private.

And, as predicted, Dell couldn't sustain the organic growth of the early years and stay true to the business model. As the company matured, it struggled to keep its spot in the marketplace. Acquisitions, in most cases, didn't ensure a high ride on the stock market, but dragged the company down, hampering innovation and forward movement.

Dell is a classic example of sprawling expansion resulting in clunkiness due to poorly executed mergers and acquisitions, which played havoc with its aspirations for growth. The lack of integration and consolidation in the areas of culture, communication, talent, structure, and strategy at Dell led to organized anarchy and clunkiness, making it difficult to work across businesses, projects, and turf.

*Clunky Culture*

Overcoming the challenge of having a clunky culture is crucial to an effective "mergers and acquisitions process and its full strength is seen during an acquisition when two divergent cultures are forced to become one."[21] Every organization has its own way of doing things, its own values and principles. Some organized anarchies—even in the absence of a merger situation—struggle with cultural mismatch and a lack of integration among the business units. There may be one way of doing business in the administrative offices, but norms may be different in the warehouse or on the shop floor. Or cultural expectations in the LA office are completely different from the Seattle office. When a merger occurs, existing problems with cultural integration within the organization can be magnified.

The other danger is that schisms may surface if culture is not part of the equation up front. This can happen when the parent or lead organization is adamant about foisting its culture on the acquired organization, leaving its members feeling imposed on or diminished. Poor or no cultural integration can lead to clunkiness.

Daimler-Benz's 1998 decision to merge with Chrysler highlights the primacy of culture within the M&A sphere. The deal initially drew praise from financial and product analysts. That said, the leaders of both companies overlooked the inherent cultural incompatibility of their units: "Chrysler had a loose, entrepreneurial culture, while Daimler-Benz had a very structured and hierarchical approach to business."[22] Because the question of culture was not dealt with early on, the association that began with such high hopes crumbled, and in 2009 Daimler sold its remaining Chrysler shares.

*Clunky Communication*

In the newly merged organization, there isn't a ready protocol for communication—not only regarding which information should be transmitted, but also how the communication is to be made—and consequently, there is a tendency toward communication break-down. At the moment when it is important to pull together as one, the inability to create a cohesive communication strategy leads the individual units and subunits to separate and purposely stand apart. Without such a strategy, the organization is susceptible to what M.L Marks and P.H. Miris call the "merger syndrome," a condition that can be partially remedied with "increased communication and employee/management interaction."[23] It is important to devise a clear communication strategy from the outset to keep the rumor mill from working overtime, and to keep not only employees but also clients and vendors in the loop about what they can expect moving forward.

Bank of America's 2008 troubled acquisition of Merrill Lynch is a potent reminder of how important communication is during a period of integration. The decision to join forces was made hastily and under pressure. In this instance, communication was the first casualty of moving so quickly. When Merrill's John Thain left Merrill before the ink was dry on the contract, employees heard about it on television instead of through internal company communication channels.[24] Not only that, employees from both sides of the new house waited in vain for months to hear basic details of the acquisition.[25] The mechanics of information flow were badly managed and amplified other problems with the deal.

## Clunky Talent Integration

Talent integration is a potential minefield, and the unsuccessful assimilation of talent can lead to a clunky organization. The acquiring or lead organization needs to be sensitive to the needs of employees on both sides of the M&A. While the players directing an M&A are frequently concerned with how things will work at the top, little thought is given to the middle—that is, the people with industry knowledge, the business know-how, and the managerial experience to execute the new, combined vision. There is a great risk that essential people will jump ship in the wake of a poorly executed M&A. Care must be taken not to duplicate activities to the degree that people feel that the value of their contribution is worthless. The ideal is to have the fusion of talent that creates synergy.

Another complication with Bank of America's acquisition of Merrill was the nonintegration of talent. Without a talent integration plan in place, many Merrill players, especially those that had attractive alternatives, chose to leave the organization. What Merrill brought to the table initially was a valuable seasoned workforce. As more people groped for the exits, the value of the merger dwindled, leaving Bank of America with an empty shell.[26]

*Clunky Structure*

The failure of coherent structural integration can contribute to increased clunkiness. In a newly enlarged organization, it is common for more than one unit to be engaged in the same activity. If the newly acquired company has a product or a market that is substantially different from the parent company, it may make sense for the acquired company to keep its own structure for the time being. If the acquired company is very much like the parent company, as in the case of a horizontal merger, a greater effort may be made to establish a unity of purpose.

The 2005 Symantec-Veritas merger never achieved the synergies it aspired to. Symantec, a leader in security software, purchased Veritas, a player in information management, for $13.5 billion to "create a more efficient company that sold a variety of products and services under the same umbrella."[27] Easier said than done. The consummation of the union between the two tech giants was long in coming. Employees stayed in their premerger roles for too long, and it took three years "to really start code sharing and maximizing the integration of products."[28] Because of an unwillingness to act as one unit and an inability for the firms to integrate satisfactorily, the two halves limped along and finally called it quits in 2016.

*Clunky Strategy*

A bad M&A experience can lead to clunky characteristics because of a disconnect between the business strategies of the parent organization and the acquired firm. For instance, sometimes a consulting firm will acquire a software company because the consulting firm's clients use the software applications. The overlap is initially evident, but the consulting firm will realize that "selling B2B applications is wholly different from managing consulting engagements."[29] Without a new, well-thought-out plan to merge strategy, effective integration is unlikely, making clunkiness more likely. Merely imposing the parent organization's strategy on the acquired firm may alienate the newly acquired employees. It is important for organizations to consider business strategies before merging, or they run the risk of encountering serious problems.

Incompatible business strategy led to the failure of eBay's 2005 acquisition of Skype. Essentially, the assumption was that Skype's technology could be leveraged to optimize the customer experience. The general idea was "that Skype would improve the auction site by giving its users a better platform for communicating."[30] However, eBay's vendors and customers were accustomed to email and didn't feel the need for a phone conversation to finalize the transaction.[31] The merger proposed to provide eBay's users with something that they didn't want and had no use for. The strategic incompatibility between customers' preference for email and their reluctance to embrace voice communication positioned the acquisition for failure.

The five challenges of M&As signal that sprawling growth, if not properly managed, can result in clunkiness and an inability to thrive. Sprawling expansion invites the creation of new processes and new structures that are not necessarily aligned with the primary organization's goals and overall mission. Intraorganizational struggles for resources and recognition may emerge. Turf skirmishes are accentuated, and it becomes unclear who's in charge of what. There is a lack of consensus and a lack of integration. There is duplication of functions. Sometimes there is lax control or oversight of resources. With improperly managed growth, the organization becomes clunky and sluggish, and inertia sets in, creating an entry point for competitors.

## The Inertia of the Myopic Tendency

Clunkiness is not the only reason why organizations experience the sluggishness of inertia. They can develop the myopic tendency. While clunkiness suggests a relatively loose system, loose relationships, and multiple, wide-ranging goals, the myopic tendency implies a tight system, tight relationships, and a focused concentration on the core intent of the organization.

In myopic organizations, internal networks are generally very strong. The linkages between the components are enmeshed, reinforcing a commonality of thought and creating a blinder effect as organizational leaders focus on re-creating what they did well in the past. Myopic organizations create a measure of safety by not readily deviating from what worked yesterday, last year, or ten years ago. Because they are so tightly integrated and committed to a common purpose, myopic organizations may have difficulty making agile adjustments.

While the clunky tendency may lead an organization to stray beyond its core mission, resulting in sluggishness and inertia, the myopic tendency can lead to inertia if the organization stays too close to its original intent. An organization known for its reputation for focusing on a specific product or specific service—clearly essential to their early growth and integral to their branding—is a likely candidate for myopia. As they mature, they experience inertia when they fail to break free of their singular focus and expand beyond their core. Organizations with the myopic tendency suffer from the blinder effect. Sometimes they are not even aware that they should adjust their thinking and shift their business model in the context of changing markets and customer needs.

Gaming-industry leader Nintendo has a history of experiencing episodes of myopia. As their competitors moved to producing consoles that doubled as home entertainment hubs with movie and music streaming with CD and Blu-ray capabilities, Nintendo remained committed to providing a creative gaming experience via a standalone gaming console. While Nintendo completely revolutionized home gaming with the Wii and Wii Fit, these wins brought about a somewhat myopic mind-set.

With the Wii U, Nintendo suffered from the blinder effect. Narrowly focused on providing the most adventurous gaming experience on a dedicated console, Nintendo failed to adapt quickly to home entertainment trends and the desires of their customer base. They expected the Wii U to be a hit based on their record of past success. However, the company went from selling 101 million Wii systems worldwide to a paltry 12.8 million units of the Wii U.[32] How did Nintendo get off track?

One of Nintendo's problems is that its competitors have seized on and improved Nintendo's innovations, such as motion-controlled games and the use of tablets to interface with the game platform.[33] While Nintendo innovates, it is becoming more difficult for it to reap the rewards of its innovations.

Another problem that Nintendo struggled with is identifying the profile of its core user. Almost "half of Nintendo Wii users described themselves as casual gamers,"[34] yet Nintendo was reluctant to give up the single-console model. With cheaper alternatives like smartphone gaming, casual players had less reason to invest in a gaming-only unit. Nintendo was being beaten in multiple arenas.

Nintendo has a tendency toward being overly focused and myopic. It succeeds, but only with constant effort. It experiences periods of sluggishness. The company has had one quick win after another, but it does not seem to thrive. While meeting some external criteria for success, the company periodically experiences myopic thinking. The Nintendo Switch is currently doing fine, one of the firm's "wins," but the company still struggles with the myopic mind-set.

The bookseller Borders Group also experienced the myopic mind-set. The organization coded itself as a retail bookstore, not as an online retailer or technology leader. Until the bitter end, Borders did not get the memo that customer reading and shopping habits were changing. The company's myopic mind-set was a contributing factor to its demise—perhaps the only factor.

Borders made the breathtaking decision to outsource its online book sales to Amazon.com. That is, a customer on the Borders website was automatically redirected to Amazon's site to make a purchase.[35] Borders's rationale was that if they were not bothered with the day-to-day management of Internet sales, they could direct their attention to their big-box stores. Consequently, online customers skipped the Borders website and went straight to Amazon. To show his gratitude for the new business, Amazon CEO Jeff Bezos sent the Borders CEO a case of champagne.[36] It was shortsighted to think that online sales were more of a nuisance than an opportunity for growth.

Similarly, Borders missed the boat on the e-reading revolution. After the 2007 launch of Amazon's Kindle, Borders didn't seem interested in the new technology (they were too busy revamping their website).[37] Two years later, rival Barnes and Noble debuted the Nook e-reader. With mounting losses, Borders did not have the cash to develop its own reader. Instead, they bought a stake in a Canadian firm to develop the Kobo e-reader. Even after it was demonstrated that there was a flourishing market for e-books, Borders treated the phenomenon as secondary to selling physical books in a real store. Another miss that Borders had was choosing to invest heavily in CD and DVD sales, exactly when Apple's iPod was taking off and the iTunes store became the dominant music seller.[38]

Borders's myopic mind-set prevented the company from thinking beyond the four walls of a physical store. They lost many opportunities to keep pace with customer tastes and shopping habits. Their lack of foresight and flexibility ultimately led to the company's failure as its leaders could not understand, let alone keep up with, the changing market.

## The Blinder Traps

While the clunky tendency leads to inertia due to sprawl and sometimes overreach, organizations with the myopic tendency experience inertia because they focus on what worked for them before. While they can adapt and improve, they do so by making repetition-based improvements.[39] In dealing with challenges, they make incremental changes, modify procedures, and focus on calculated adjustments. Myopic organizations continuously reinforce their comfort zone by living in the past. They are not necessarily blind to their environment or customers, but they take a myopic approach in that their capacity to make adjustments relies on prior experience.[40]

Organizations with myopic tendencies are inclined toward sluggishness and inertia because of their reluctance to move outside of the proverbial box. They become affected by the blinder mind-set. The blinder mind-set is the consequence of a number of cognitive traps that reinforce the myopic tendency.

*Status Quo Trap*

Organizations too satisfied with how things are going can be seduced by the status quo trap.[41] The status quo trap is set when times are good—sales are up and the financials are solid. By not looking ahead to see what's around the corner, the firm isn't committing time or resources into developing the next generation of innovative ideas. There is a tendency for leaders to stay very much in the moment and not spend time worrying about tomorrow. When the wind shifts—market demand drops or the economy weakens—organizations lured into the status quo trap are not able to exercise flexibility and adapt. They haven't nurtured the new ideas that could help them get over a rough patch.

The status quo trap tripped up Nintendo. Nintendo was moving from strength to strength in the gaming industry. With the Wii as a qualified success, the company was lulled into a sense of complacency. Customers loved the first-generation Wii, so why wouldn't they get on board with Wii U? This is exactly what the company was thinking.

Nintendo president Tatsumi Kimishima told shareholders, "In an internal sales representative meeting someone projected that we would sell close to 100 million Wii U systems worldwide. . . . The thinking was that because the Wii sold so well, the Wii U would follow suit."[42] The Wii U did not follow suit, and the reasons why are up for debate. Was there trouble with the audio port? Was the catalog of games too small? Was something subpar with the graphics? Was it a branding problem? Whatever the precise reasons, Wii U did not do as well as anticipated, largely because of the status quo trap, and the false expectation that past success was a blueprint for the future.

*Bailing-Too-Late Trap*

The bailing-too-late trap is when an organization makes a big investment in a venture that just doesn't work out—but they are reluctant to pull out.[43] Rather than recognizing the mistake and cutting bait when the losses are still manageable, leaders are compelled to throw even more money into the sinking project, hoping to keep it afloat. It is hard to abandon a project that has a lot of sunk costs because there is always a faint hope of eking out some kind of success (even when the Magic 8-Ball confirms the worst: "Outlook not so good").

Sony Corporation is a leader in entertainment, financial services, and most notably consumer electronics. In 2001, Sony engaged in a joint venture with Ericsson to enter the telecommunications market under the banner Sony Ericsson. In 2012, then-CEO Howard Stringer led Sony's acquisition of the unit for $1.5 billion to focus on smartphones and potentially benefit from synergy opportunities. At the time, Stringer said, "We can use our content as a weapon to drive the sales of our products. None of our competitors has more content—movie and music studios, video games—and the fact that we have tied all this together makes us very powerful."[44] However, concrete plans on how to exploit collaborative opportunities were not developed, and Sony found it difficult to make a profit in the electronics business and achieve the desired synergies. In 2013, Sony faced significant losses in its electronics division to the tune of $8.5 billion. Investment banking firm Jefferies reported that "electronics is [Sony's] Achilles' heel and, in our view, it is worth zero. . . . It needs to exit most electronics markets."[45] It is apparent that Sony is failing in its strategy to drive content synergies between its consumer electronics products.

Stringer's successor, Kazuo Hirai, reaffirmed Sony's earlier allegiance to the consumer electronics business. Sony was in thrall to the bailing-too-late trap. As late as 2017 Hirai expressed the opinion that Sony's participation in the mobile business "would continue regardless of its ability to take market share from Apple and Samsung."[46] Hirai is positioning Sony to take advantage of future opportunities by maintaining the mobile business and keeping its relationships with retailers and carriers. While Sony may be preparing for future gains, it is most likely harboring the so-far unrequited hope to extract a shred of success from its venture into the mobile business.

*Overreaching Trap*

When a company proposes to enter a new market or provide a new product or service but doesn't possess the requisite competencies, skills, or material necessary to execute, they unwittingly trigger the over-reaching trap.[47] If the company is in over its head—if its aspirations do not mesh with the current reality—they are going to have more than a fair chance at failure. Although broadening horizons and expanding product lines are admirable ideas in theory, they are terrible, and possibly very costly, ideas when the organization does not have the immediate capacity to execute.

GE Capital is the financial services arm of global conglomerate GE. The unit, which "began life ever so humbly in the 1930s as a captive finance subsidiary formed to bankroll GE's washing machines and other household appliances,"[48] grew into a behemoth with its tentacles in areas related to insurance, real estate, finance, and banking. By the 1990s, GE Capital generated a significant portion of GE's profits.[49] Despite GE Capital's profitability, it took its parent into businesses that were a significant departure from its core competencies and skills in management and global manufacturing, making it vulnerable to the whims of the market.

Fast forward to 2008 and GE was confronted with "a near-death moment...when it needed almost $60 billion of government guarantees for its debt to stay afloat."[50] GE had to cut dividends in 2009 for the first time since 1938 and became subject to financial regulations as a lender under the Dodd-Frank Wall Street Reform and Consumer Protection Act. To move forward, then-CEO Jeffrey Immelt knew that GE "must rely more on making physical products and less on financial engineering,"[51] and he led the effort to divest GE Capital. In a public statement Immelt noted, "We are confident that creating a simpler GE will position us to deliver superior outcomes around our core capabilities."[52] As of 2017, GE is on pace to generate more than 90 percent of its profits from its industrial operations,[53] proof that the company is trying to extract itself from the overreaching trap.

*Short-Term Trap*
Sometimes organizations confuse short-term wins with positive long-term gains. Short-term wins are great, but if they are pursued at the expense of long-term success, then it's a trap. The short-term trap stems from striving to satisfy customer desires with traditional—and expected—products or services. Organizations that are snagged by the short-term trap miss big opportunities. The short-term trap shares some characteristics of the status quo trap, but without the sense of complacency. In either case, the result is the same—no new products in the pipeline. In the case of the short-term trap, there is activity. Customer needs are being met, but there is no investment in and no thought to the future.

Kodak is famous for falling prey to the short-term trap. At one time Kodak was a tremendously innovative company and advanced photography from studio portraits to family snapshots to motion pictures. Kodak's fortunes were tied to servicing film-dependent customers: "The gross margins on film sales approached 70 percent... Kodak was selling a lot of film, and it was making...a ton of money."[54] The mentality of its corporate leadership centered on preserving its primary source of cash flow: film photography. Satisfying this customer need occurred at the expense of fulfilling Kodak's potential for becoming an innovator in digital photography. For Kodak, the short-term trap was created by a combination of excessive customer alignment, narrow focus, and blinkered leadership, which eventually led to it filing for Chapter 11.

*Overthinking Trap*

Organizations that embark on the endless journey of spending too much time analyzing, discussing, researching, and testing a new idea, without getting anything off the ground, are victims of the overthinking trap. With the overthinking trap, teams spend so much time processing an idea that they never achieve anything. No one—neither team members nor the leader—is prepared to risk taking that important first step of transforming the idea into a concrete innovation. Consequently, the organization wastes precious time and money, throwing away the opportunity to move toward real innovation.

For Kodak, the leap from the short-term trap to the overthinking trap was like jumping from the frying pan into the fire. Kodak's troubled launch of the Advantix hybrid film and digital camera, which allowed users to choose the best shot to print, showed the perils of the deliberation trap. It took over twenty years—from the introduction of "filmless photography"[55] (which was greeted with a degree of bewilderment and puzzlement) to the 1996 product release. Kodak spent too much time and $500 million deliberating and analyzing, and consequently was too late to be a player in the digital age.[56]

These cognitive traps create myopic thinking that leads to inertia, preventing organizations from reaching their potential. Such traps are cognitive blinders that steer leaders away from taking bold steps, pulling the plug, redirecting their efforts to their strengths, favoring the present over the future, and taking too long to launch an idea because there needs to be another meeting. Leaders of organizations of all sizes should not ignore the potential danger of these traps. Once a trap is triggered, even well-established organizations can slip down a sinkhole of myopia and be stymied by inertia. The leadership challenge is to identify and disable the traps that can prevent the movement of ideas to execution.

▲  ▲  ▲

Why do organizations sometimes get stuck? What makes them sluggish? There are two fundamental reasons why organizations experience inertia. The first source of inertia is the clunky tendency. The clunky tendency is usually found in complex organizations, with complicated structures, overlapping missions, unintegrated units, confused lines of authority, and a general sense of organized anarchy. The second source of inertia is the myopic tendency. Organizations with myopic tendencies are trapped in old ways of doing things and old business models. Clunky or myopic tendencies do not immediately result in organizational failure, but they do result in sluggishness, a slow slope that may lead to failure. Having understood why the organization is sluggish and having evaluated the organization's clunky and myopic tendencies, the pragmatic leadership challenge is to overcome the resulting inertia and ensure that the organization reaches its potential.

## REACHING POTENTIAL: LEADING FOR DISCOVERY AND DELIVERY

All organizations encounter some degree of inertia. Inertia is manifested by sluggish discovery or sluggish delivery. The leaders of organizations that actively work toward breaking inertia understand that to thrive and reach their potential it is important to continuously engage in robust discovery and focused delivery. They ensure that organizations and units can adapt to new trends and deliver concrete results and innovation. To do so, leaders have to lead with flexibility and agility and create collective organizational synergy. They don't dig holes they can't get out of—that is, they don't tie themselves to specific products, processes, or customers—but they make sure their organization stays ahead of the game.

Amazon started in 1994 as an online bookstore (and, keeping to the script, in Jeff Bezos's garage),[57] where in theory, a virtually unlimited stock of books could be on offer. The idea of selling books online—at a time when the concept of "online" was a novelty for the public—was highly innovative. Customers agreed that Bezos had a good idea, and within two months Amazon's sales were averaging $20,000/week.[58] Bezos did not stop at selling books. Practically anything can be purchased via Amazon.com, any product, as the logo suggests, from A to Z.

The customer is central to Amazon's philosophy, and "customer obsession" is the first of Amazon's expanding (now fourteen) Leadership Principles.[59] The company is always thinking of ways to enhance and improve the customer experience and fulfill customer needs. Always innovating, Amazon continues to develop a varied line of products and platforms from the Kindle Reader, Amazon Web Services, and Amazon Video, to Amazon Studios and Amazon Game Studios. Not only does Amazon provide the platform for delivering media, it is now creating content for video games and what used to be called television.[60]

How does Amazon do it?

For Bezos, the discovery phase is very important, and that means experimentation: "Experiments are key to innovation because they rarely turn out as you expect and you learn so much. We've tried to reduce the cost of doing experiments so that we can do more of them. If you can increase the number of experiments you try from a hundred to a thousand, you dramatically increase the number of innovations you produce."[61]

Bezos is willing to support bold experiments where failure is part of the equation.[62] The Fire Phone did not work out so well, and neither did Amazon Auctions. That said, Amazon is working on the drone delivery of packages—and space travel![63]

Were it not for Bezos's energized vision, Amazon could have easily become a clunky organization—and experienced growth in fits and starts in unrelated areas. Or Amazon could have veered into myopic territory and shared the same doomed destiny as Borders Group. Amazon adeptly avoided the pitfalls of both clunkiness and myopia and constantly identifies new opportunities to enhance the lives of its customers. Its diversified growth is defined by better serving the customer. Under Bezos's leadership, Amazon incorporates the right amount of "looseness" that allows its different divisions the flexibility to run their operations effectively without adding layers of bureaucracy. At the same time, its customer-centered mission permeates the entire organization and is the string that binds its disparate initiatives together. Amazon is a truly thriving organization with a common mission and culture that adapts to new trends, fosters new ideas, and finds new markets.

Google is another example of an organization unencumbered by inertia. The organization is still relatively new and fresh-faced compared to enduring brands such as Colgate, Brooks Brothers, and the Ford Motor Company: "Pause to consider that just 15 years ago, Google's search engine, now used globally over 100 billion times a month, didn't exist. Products most of us take for granted, including Google Maps, Gmail, Translator, Google Earth, and Android all were created since 1998 when Larry Page and Sergey Brin cofounded the firm with the soaring ambition of making the world's information available to everyone."[64] Google is constantly finding areas where it can innovate, and provide solutions—some slicker than others—that users will appreciate.

Larry Page leads the organization to reach its potential. The head of Google, he and Sergey Brin made the announcement in 2015 that a new enterprise—Alphabet—would be created to house Google and its sundry businesses. Why would they tinker with something that seemed to be working so well? In a blog post, Page explains: "We've long believed that over time companies tend to get comfortable doing the same thing, just making incremental changes. But in the technology industry, where revolutionary ideas drive the next big growth areas, you need to be a bit uncomfortable to stay relevant."[65] And to do that, Page needed the freedom that a new structure would give him to "boil new oceans, such as *transportation, connectivity,* and *life itself.*"[66] The creation of Alphabet was a decisive move that ensured that the organization would remain fluid and expand its ability to discover new practices, products, and business models while at the same time tinkering with its current businesses. The individual businesses can operate with a degree of fluidity, and they can better explore their individual external challenges, without having to filter information and decisions through a clunky organization. In fact, Alphabet is the antidote to clunkiness.

When an organization grows as quickly as Google did, its many divisions will hit different levels of maturity at different times. It would be unreasonable to expect that the component parts would grow at the same rate and face the same levels of uncertainty, or that success

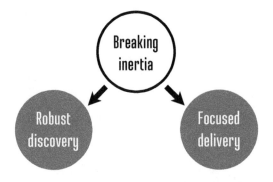

can be measured with the same yardstick.

Google-now-Alphabet has grown significantly but is still nimble. It understands its customers and can still surprise them with delivery of novel solutions and products. It is a fluid organization that stays ahead of the game and sets the bar for its competitors. Like Amazon, Alphabet is unencumbered by inertia and reaches its potential.

The leadership of Amazon and Alphabet are visionaries and pragmatic leaders. When pragmatic leaders are on top of industry trends and have a passion for experimentation, the organizational capacity to discover is transformed. When pragmatic leaders understand how to establish connections with the right people and move their agenda to fruition, it translates into the organizational capability of delivery. To meet potential and avoid the traps of inertia caused by clunkiness and myopia, pragmatic leaders must support robust discovery and focused delivery. To ensure robust discovery, pragmatic leaders must create an environment where ideas can ferment. They need to establish the organizational ecosystem where new trends, new directions, and new ideas can be explored, and where experimentation with prototypes can take place. To ensure focused delivery, pragmatic leaders must create an environment where units and individuals can reach across divisions, turf, and silos to collectively move ideas ahead and make sure that flexibility and focus sustain the momentum to drive implementation.

## Robust Discovery

Robust discovery is necessary to reach potential. For leaders to ensure that organizations engage in robust discovery, they must have the contextual competence to explore their environment and pick up cues, hints, and trends that may reveal obstacles, challenges, and opportunities. Robust discovery also demands that leaders have the ideational competence to lead for collective innovation, making sure that the environment is open to experimentation and safe risk-taking, to ensure that ideas move through a process that leads to prototypes and concrete results. Organizations that engage in robust discovery have leaders who are both contextually competent and ideationally competent. As such, discovery necessitates that pragmatic leaders initiate exploration and encourage ideation to make sure that their organization stays ahead of the curve.

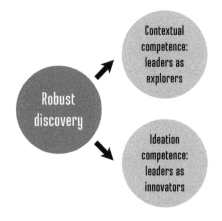

**Contextual Competence: Leaders as Explorers**

Leaders who push their organizations ahead are constantly searching for new stimuli and opportunities. Leaders as explorers are aware of the internal and external stimuli that may indicate the need to make adjustments or move in new directions. They perpetually cast nets into the environment, with the expectation that some bits of information, some sense of a trend, or some perception of changing customer interest will signal an important new direction. Pragmatic leaders with contextual competence analyze the environment, pick up trends that others may have overlooked, and are aware of emerging competition.

With contextual competence, leaders become sensitive to the environment in which they operate, becoming aware of changing markets, changing industries, new trends, changing customer demands, changing technology, and changing political contexts. They are constantly engaged in agile exploration, anticipating new challenges, new directions, new competitors, new opportunities, and the various obstacles that could hamper or enhance their capacity to move things ahead.

As illustrated above, the Dell organization has a tendency toward clunkiness. Michael Dell's leadership approach is famously conservative, and he is not known for being quick to spot or act on key trends and changes in the industry.

When customers were moving away from personal computers to mobile phones and tablets, he preferred to follow a cautious approach to preserve Dell's market position. Former CEO Kevin Rollins wanted to acquire EMC, which provides data storage and information security, to give Dell a little more product diversity. Rollins recalls: "I couldn't get Michael to agree. . . . He was worried that it would be too destabilizing for the company."[67] Rollins eventually won the argument, as Dell acquired EMC in 2016. That said, Michael Dell's lack of contextual competence had the effect of flatlining Dell's growth.

RadioShack also suffered because its leaders failed to understand changing customer preferences and behavior. Started in 1921 in Boston, RadioShack had one location specializing in gear for amateur radio hobbyists—who were in almost constant need of parts to build and maintain their equipment. By 1939 the company moved into mail order and entered the burgeoning stereo market. By the 1960s, it misread cues, and was struggling financially when it was revived by Charles Tandy, who was arguably the force of the company's success, at least up until his death in 1978.[68]

Through the 1970s and '80s, Radio Shack (it lost the space and became "RadioShack" in a 1999 rebranding effort) found a market in CB radios, home phones (after the breakup of Ma Bell), and the TRS-80 computer. By 2011, most of RadioShack's sales were attributable to smartphones.[69] By 2015, the company was looking for a lifeline out of bankruptcy, and Sprint threw them a rope, with a deal to share the stores that hadn't yet been closed.[70]

A onetime employee sums up the challenges that RadioShack faced before the bottom fell out:

> This is a consumer technology business that is built to work perfectly in the year 1975. The Internet comes around, and this, being a technology company, is expected to move on it aggressively and know what it's doing, except basically nobody really understood the Internet for a very long time. So they whiffed big a few times. Then the iPhone came around and rendered half the stuff RadioShack sold completely redundant. This company needed to become something radically different a decade ago. I just don't think it knows how to be anything else.[71]

RadioShack's leaders focused on revamping branding or restructuring efforts instead of keeping an eye on the competition and evolving with changing customer preferences. Their discovery was sluggish. They had not developed the contextual competence to engage in deep exploration.

Jeff Bezos is a skilled explorer: "While surfing the Internet in search of new ventures . . . [he] came across the statistic that World Wide Web usage was growing by 2,300 percent a month. Bezos immediately recognized the expansive possibilities of selling online and began exploring the entrepreneurial possibilities of developing an Internet business."[72] From the instant he had the idea of an online bookstore, he stayed on top of current trends and figured out how to make the environment work for Amazon. Bezos continues to lead the company in exploration. Riding the wave of booming drone technology, Amazon has been experimenting with drones that are intended "to deliver packages to people's homes and offices in under 30 minutes."[73]

Bezos's external and internal awareness—his contextual competence—makes it possible for the organization to exploit the latest technology and develop internal capabilities not only to serve the future needs of customers but also to stay nimble and ahead of the competition. Amazon continues to be contextually agile, and is constantly seeking new directions and new ways to satisfy customer needs.

The leaders of Netflix are also explorers. When Netflix was getting off the ground, Blockbuster was the market leader. Blockbuster's business model was to rent VHS tapes and later DVDs to customers at a relatively low rate, but to charge outlandish late fees, which were the company's bread and butter.

Netflix CEO Reed Hastings realized that this win-lose model where a business made money when customers paid fines wasn't sustainable.[74] Netflix's innovation was to offer subscriptions rather than to charge for single rentals of DVDs. Customers liked this model because they had the freedom to keep media indefinitely without racking up late fees. Hastings showed contextual competence in understanding what the customers wanted from their movie-rental experience.

Initially Netflix mailed DVDs to customers, but Hastings knew he could leverage the changing technological trends and deliver product online. He did not hesitate to pivot from a physical model of distribution to online video streaming. Hastings's contextual competence, his ability to understand both changing customer expectations and the power of advancing technology, propelled Netflix into becoming one of today's largest entertainment companies.

As these examples show, to break inertia it is essential for pragmatic leaders to have the contextual competence to explore. Without exploration, there is an increased probability that the organization will experience sluggishness. Exploration opens the door to new directions and new niches.

### Ideational Competence: Leaders as Innovators

While it's important for organizations to have leaders who try to stay ahead of the game, have an awareness of the environment, and explore the context to foster new ideas and face challenges, having contextual competence alone is not enough to overcome sluggish discovery. Leaders who are aware of the external possibilities and challenges but do not have the ideational competence to transfer those challenges into actionable, concrete innovation, change agendas, and prototypes can drive their organizations into sluggish territory. Leaders who are innovators can take the signals and trends picked up through exploration and convert them to concrete possibilities and specific initiatives. They have the ideational competence to nurture the collective synergy of the organization to follow up on the initial insights and create real possibilities. They make sure that their organization can move from insight to innovation.

Microsoft showed signs of being clunky and a bit myopic as it matured. Kurt Eichenwald notes, "Microsoft failed repeatedly to jump on emerging technologies because of the company's fealty to Windows and Office."[75] Steve Stone, a founder of Microsoft's technology group, echoes this assessment, "Windows was the god—everything had to work with Windows."[76]

Microsoft had many false starts when attempting to come up with a search engine that could go head-to-head with Google. At the end of the tunnel was Bing. When it was released in 2009, "the unit working on online search had become encrusted with Microsoft bureaucracy and the usual destructiveness that came along with it."[77] Microsoft's leaders did not focus on continuous ideation to ensure expeditious innovation. While progress was made, it was constantly hampered by the organization's tendency toward inertia.

Google's culture empowers and encourages employees to come up with new ideas. When he became CEO of Google in 2001, Eric Schmidt instituted the now-famous 70:20:10 rule to guide the innovation process.[78] Using the formula, technical employees ideally should "spend 70 percent of [their] time on the core business, 20 percent on related projects, and 10 percent on unrelated new business."[79] Schmidt notes that while the ratio applies to management, the content is a little different: "We spend 70 percent of our time on core search and ads. We spend 20 percent on adjacent businesses, ones related to the core businesses in some interesting way. Examples of that would be Google News, Google Earth, and Google Local. And then 10 percent of our time should be on things that are truly new."[80]

This framework not only encourages innovation but also helps the organization choose which products to develop so that it doesn't lose focus on its core strengths. Google channels innovation in the right direction because of the culture created by its leadership. Leaders at Google have the ideational competence to promote the discovery of new innovative ideas.

Like Google's leaders, Tesla's have the ideational competence to promote a culture of innovative thinking, starting with the employees they recruit. Generally, Tesla recruits the top problem solvers. CIO Jay Vigayan reports, "Elon [Musk] doesn't settle for good or very good. He wants the best. So he asks job candidates what kinds of complex problems they've solved before and he wants details."[81] By targeting and recruiting the "best," Musk promotes out-of-the-box thinking. Musk further promotes Tesla's innovation culture through its unique employee rewards strategy. Like recruitment, bonuses and promotions are tied to problem-solving capability, "built around a 1-to-5 rating system, with 4 and 5 being 'great' and 'phenomenal,' respectively."[82] A 5 is reserved for those who have done "something that makes the company better or the product better."[83] Musk's ideational competence ensures that good ideas are brought forward to prototype and that team players are rewarded for their contributions.

Proctor and Gamble overcame sluggishness because of the approach its leaders took toward innovation. In 2000 P&G was unable to launch innovative products into the market quickly enough, despite heavy R&D investment. To remedy the situation, the newly appointed CEO A.G. Lafley launched the "connect and develop innovation model," which enabled P&G to "identify promising ideas throughout the world and apply [their]... R&D, manufacturing, marketing, and purchasing capabilities... to create better and cheaper products, faster."[84] This open innovation model offers an opportunity for outside developers and university researchers to get their ideas noticed by P&G. Products incubated by the connect and develop initiative range from Swiffer Dusters to the Crest SpinBrush. Lafley's willingness to expand innovation opportunities allows the organization to launch new products and keep consumers excited and engaged.

Pragmatic leaders who are innovators display their ideational competence by making sure that initial ideas are incubated and developed, and result in real innovation. They make sure that information is shared and the culture of innovation is positive. They lead for ideation. Without this focus, initial insights that emerge from exploration may not result in concrete innovation and change.

## Focused Delivery

While robust discovery ensures sensitivity to new trends and allows for the emergence of new ideas, this is only half of the solution to the inertia dilemma. The second challenge pragmatic leaders face in breaking inertia is focused delivery. Once the ideas take some concrete form, can they be put in place and implemented? Can organizational leaders gain support to go the distance? Do organizational leaders have the capacity to sustain the momentum necessary to get results? Discovery—no matter how thorough—is not a guarantee of delivery.

Pragmatic leaders who deliver have the political competence to campaign for support and the managerial competence to sustain momentum. In an organizational context, delivery is often determined by the political competence of leaders—their ability to campaign for their ideas and gain support—and their managerial competence—their ability to sustain forward movement. Politically competent leaders campaign for their innovation or change agenda and push it through the organizational maze. Managerially competent leaders sustain momentum and make sure that the ball is not dropped. Leaders in sluggish organizations may have impeccable discovery, but they may stumble when it comes to making those good ideas a reality.

## Political Competence: Leaders as Campaigners
Political competence—the capacity to work across divisions, sections, and product lines—is essential to breaking inertia. Politically

competent leaders appreciate the importance of assembling the right support, mustering cooperation, and forming the crucial alliances necessary to move ideas and challenges through the eye of the needle. They understand that they need to bring stakeholders together to overcome the challenges of turf, the entrenchment of inertia, and the resistance to change. Campaigning for support by creating linkages and building coalitions is essential to gaining traction that ensures focused delivery. To overcome the inertia of clunky and myopic organizations, leaders must have the political competence to drive for execution.

Steve Jobs was a great visionary, but he learned the hard way about the necessity of campaigning for support for his agenda. In 1985, Jobs's pet project was the "second-generation Mac, the Macintosh Office."[85] Former Apple CEO John Sculley recalled that the product had been "'ridiculed' as a 'toy,' a victim of too much ambition for the relatively small amount of computing power then available."[86] Jobs asked Sculley to drop the price and move some advertising from the Apple 2 to prop up the Macintosh Office, and Sculley insisted that the poor product reception had "nothing to do with the price or the advertising."[87] Jobs disagreed, and ultimately they both went to the board (separately) to make the case for their position, and the board decided to go with Sculley, precipitating Jobs's departure from the company synonymous with his name.[88] Jobs neglected to engage in the fundamental political campaigning that could have saved his ideas—and his job—from the ash heap.

Indra Nooyi, the current chairman and CEO of Pepsi, is widely regarded as a good negotiator. Nooyi's career progressed at an admirable rate, and in 2006 she was declared one of two finalists—along with her colleague Mike White—to succeed Steven Reinemund as CEO.[89] After being appointed CEO, she paid her former rival a visit and offered him compensation that nearly matched hers,[90] creating in the process a coalition and a right-hand man. She knew that being successful in her new job required the support of her colleagues.

Nooyi's political competence enabled her to circumvent the attack by investor and activist shareholder Nelson Peltz in July 2013.[91] In 2007 Peltz intervened at Kraft, forcing it to acquire Cadbury and split the newly combined company into two entities. He had a similar demand for Nooyi: have PepsiCo acquire Mondelēz International (of which Peltz was a significant shareholder) and then split PepsiCo into two entities, one focused on beverages and the other on food.

In the context of the threat, Nooyi showed her political competence by coalescing with the board to come up with a new strategy that would defuse Peltz's intentions. To create a buffer strategy, she came up with a new strategic focus of "performance with purpose" that included shifting to healthier products and moving into new markets such as Brazil, China, India, and eastern Europe.[92] While such a transformation takes time to show results, with her board's support she managed to maintain focus on this new strategic direction. Having a deep support base and forming long-lasting alliances is the result of hard-won trust and a transparent, candid communication style, indicative of her political competence as a first-rate campaigner.

When Bob Iger succeeded Michael Eisner as the CEO of Disney, he repeatedly demonstrated his political competence. He understood that the key to developing a collaborative relationship among Disney, Pixar, and Apple was his personal relationship with Steve Jobs. He correctly perceived that he needed Jobs on his side for his idea of a renewed and expanded aggressive media partnership to attract the initial support it needed to become a reality. Before the announcement was made that he had been tapped to be Disney's incoming CEO in 2005, Iger mobilized a campaign to mend the company's ailing relationship with Pixar by personally reaching out to Jobs. Hinting at the possibilities that the future held, Iger communicated that Disney's dealings with Pixar would no longer be business as usual. Jobs gave Iger the benefit of the doubt, and asked him to fly to Apple headquarters to see if collaboration was possible. Pixar cofounder Ed Catmull recalls, "Steve recognized that in Bob he actually had a partner.... In the subsequent years they thought of each other as true partners."[93]

Because Iger's initial attempt to build a coalition with Jobs was successful, they were able to transform their relationship and widen the scope of their cooperation. When iTunes started to offer video in late 2005, Disney was one of the first content creators in line, and released ABC programming such as *Lost* and *Desperate Housewives* on this platform.[94] The apex of the Iger-Jobs coalition was Disney's 2006 acquisition of Pixar. "As part of the deal, Catmull and [Pixar cofounder John] Lasseter took over all of Disney's animation division. Jobs, the majority shareholder in Pixar, became Disney's largest shareholder."[95] This acquisition paved the way for the new golden age of animated movies, such as *Cars*, *Wall-E*, and *Frozen*. By mobilizing Jobs's support, Iger showed that he was a campaigner with the political competence necessary to lead Disney's animation studios to renewed success. Achieving the essential integration between media and technology, he successfully moved Disney's media operations. Since then, the company has enjoyed a string of record yearly profits.

The leaders in these illustrations are campaigners, with a demonstrated capacity to gain support for their position. Without their capacity to campaign, work the maze, and gain support, it is unlikely that their discovery—their good ideas—would achieve delivery. Whether Nooyi, Iger, or Jobs, the message is clear. Pragmatic leaders understand that since priorities are mixed, agendas differ, and resources are limited, they have to use their political competence to convince, persuade, and gain support. To overcome resistance and inertia—and to deliver—they must be superb campaigners.

**Managerial Competence: Leaders as Sustainers**

The delivery of innovative ideas takes time—and sometimes the process is longer and more arduous than expected. No matter how long it takes to deliver a new product, the effort needs to be sustained and managed. Pragmatic leaders who break inertia rarely drop the ball. Once ideas have garnered support and some initial traction, these leaders use their managerial competence to sustain the commitment of key units and individuals to move the project forward and make sure that it's not stalled or sidetracked. That is, they are managerially competent.

Pragmatic leaders understand that to move forward and implement requires that they keep focus on sustaining momentum. That is, they enhance and reinforce the commitment of their teams. In a world in which it is easy to get distracted by multiple demands, bureaucratic bottlenecks, and obstacles, organizations that are successful in breaking inertia have leaders who can establish and manage positive synergy and sustain forward movement.

Consider the role Jeff Bezos played while the team was working on Kindle: "Bezos, internalizing hundreds of data points, believed millions of people would want a crisp e-book reader that could download any book in 60 seconds or less. He set that delivery target without getting pinned down by technical issues about the right compression ratios or transmission speeds for book files. Engineers were free to solve technical challenges as they saw fit. They just needed to make it right for consumers."[96] He well understood that to move ahead, he could delineate the direction, but not overspecify the technical execution.

Bezos understands that commitment can wane, no matter how enthusiastic the initial reaction. It took years to build the right hardware for Kindle, and the team easily could have lost its momentum. However, Bezos supported them and sustained their motivation on the project. When asked how much this venture was going to cost, Bezos asked, "How much do we have?"[97] He was totally committed to the Kindle project and went to great lengths to support the team. Bezos is a sustainer who has the managerial competence to deliver.

As shown by the development of the iPad, Steve Jobs understood that implementation and moving ideas to reality was often a long game, requiring managerial competence and continuous focus. He knew that without leadership commitment to sustaining momentum, the iPad would be dropped. When the device was launched with fanfare on January 27, 2010, Jobs asked the audience, "Is there room for a third category of device [between the iPhone and the Macbook laptop]?"[98] The initial response was a head-scratcher—"customers knew instinctively that they needed a phone and a laptop...the only tablets they had ever seen were devices they didn't want."[99] By the time the product was available for delivery in April, sales were brisk. By 2011, the iPad was recognized as the game changer that it really was: "But the iPad was turning five industries upside down. It was changing the way consumers bought and read books, newspapers, and magazines—as well as the way they watched movies and television. Revenues from these businesses totaled about $250 billion, or about 2 percent of U.S. GDP."[100]

For all the fanfare at its launch, the iPad had languished in development at Apple since 2002. Unhappy with the technology at that time, Jobs turned his attention to the iPhone. Once the smartphone was released in 2007, iPad development was brought back online, and some of the technologies used for the iPhone were integrated into the new device. The success of the iPhone was motivation for the engineers who were assigned to work on the iPad.

Jobs routinely assigned top performers to plum roles on breakthrough projects. Everyone knew who the best players were, and recruitment to a priority project attested to their expertise. By appointing the very best to the most sought-after positions, Jobs not only recognized and rewarded performance, but also sustained their desire to continue performing well for the company.[101]

He also promoted a culture of responsibility, hewed to the philosophy of simplicity, and engaged in constant course correction. At Apple, "there is never any confusion as to who is responsible for what"[102] and the responsible party is noted on meeting agendas. As for simplicity, "there aren't any committees at Apple, the concept of general management is frowned on."[103] There is also simplicity in Apple's approach to product development, using the fewest number of team members possible to get the job done. Apple's ability as a billion-dollar company to behave and react like a startup can be attributed to its constant course correction. One insider notes, "If the executive team decides to change direction, it's instantaneous."[104] Steve Jobs created a tight yet nimble and patently nonsluggish framework where ideation was possible and innovation flourished.

To sustain momentum, Jobs was politically astute, concerned about counterpolitical forces, understanding the importance of keeping the commitment of others. He understood that successful product innovation and execution, such as the iPad, depended on keeping the power players in his corner. Jobs listened to his executives and took their ideas into consideration—but not without some sparks. He didn't shrink from an argument: "he loved to argue, and...[had a] habit of 'throw[ing] you off balance by suddenly adopting your position as his own, without acknowledging that he ever thought differently.'"[105] Jobs's ability to understand and incorporate the ideas of others allowed him to sustain their support and create the most innovative product possible.

Jobs and Bezos understood that if delivery were to occur, it is essential that the organization's leaders sustain the forward movement. No matter how good the idea or how much political traction it has, pragmatic leaders use managerial competence to sustain a sense of collective concern and continuous commitment that ensures final implementation. Without leaders who are committed to sustaining momentum, organizations are likely to be trapped and slowed down by clunky structures or myopic tendencies, resulting in good ideas dying on the vine.

▲  ▲  ▲

The chart below offers a framework for organizations to break inertia:

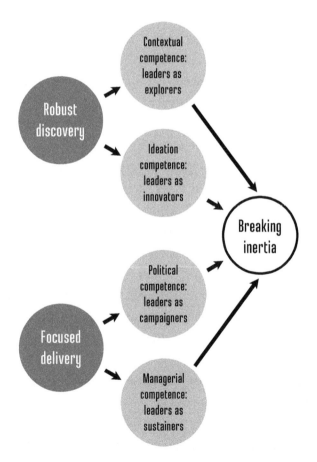

For the last thirty years, there has been much emphasis on many dimensions of organizational change and innovation. That said, the key to overcoming the type of inertia that is brought about by clunky or myopic tendencies is leadership. For all the reengineering, restructuring, refiguring, and macro adjustments that are often pursued and prescribed by consultants and academics, in the final analysis, an organization will reach its potential and overcome inertia when its leaders focus on the pragmatic steps that can be taken to ensure robust discovery and focused delivery. Doing so allows them to situate their organization as a hub of new ideas, while simultaneously giving them the capacity to deliver on these new ideas.

Inertia can be broken when individual leaders at all levels of an organization have the contextual competence to explore and the ideational competence to innovate, ensuring robust discovery. Leaders also need to develop the political competence to campaign and the managerial competence to sustain momentum to ensure focused delivery. Without these core pragmatic leadership skills, breaking inertia is impossible.

# 2

# LEADING FOR ROBUST DISCOVERY

## EXPLORE THE CONTEXT

Many organizations fail because their leaders are not sensitive to subtle changes in the environment and, consequently, are not able to make adjustments in a timely manner. How often has it been reported that a given organization missed a trend, ignored a competitor, or didn't read a market opportunity?

Organizations are embedded in their environment, which is the relevant contextual universe of customers, partners, clients, competitors, government regulation, changing technologies, shifting markets, and, all too often, a nearly infinite array of ideas, opportunities, and challenges. For some organizations, the environmental context is vast, while for others it is much more narrow. It is a world of strong signals, weak signals, and noise.

Organizations that break inertia have leaders who have the contextual competence to act as explorers. Explorers are leaders who can explore, mine, and analyze the context of the environment where the work is conducted. They recognize the importance of agile exploration of markets, competitors, changing customers, shifting technologies, or political upheavals that may influence the future direction of their organization. Organizations that break inertia are permeable open systems: their leaders scan their environment and pick up bits of information that identify potential challenges, opportunities, and difficulties. Their leaders have the contextual competence not displayed by leaders in organizations trapped by inertia.

The leadership of BlackBerry (known as RIM prior to 2013) moved slowly off the mark in response to the iPhone. The BlackBerry device was "by modern standards . . . basic—no touchscreen or even colour—but it was the first handset properly to combine phone calls with full email support, a web browser and a digital calendar."[1]

As revolutionary as the BlackBerry was, its market dominance left its leaders unprepared for the introduction of the iPhone, which as Steve Jobs promised, was intended to "reinvent the phone."[2] The iPhone "brings together several features of the iPod, digital camera, smart phones and even portable computing to one device, with a widescreen display and an innovative input method."[3] That innovative method was the human finger, in lieu of a stylus or a traditional keyboard.

The initial response at RIM was to think that they lost their mobile services client (AT&T) to Apple, but they were less concerned with the performance of the iPhone. Larry Conlee, chief operating officer for product development and manufacturing, summed up the consensus at RIM: "[The iPhone] wasn't a threat to RIM's core business. . . . It wasn't secure. It had rapid battery drain and a lousy [digital] keyboard."[4] RIM felt BlackBerry customers would continue to value security over nearly limitless access to YouTube videos, and RIM executives were cynical about the iPhone's potential: "By all rights the product should have failed, but it did not," said David Yach, RIM's chief technology officer. RIM executives were late in realizing that Apple disrupted the market by turning the smartphone "from something that was purely functional to a product that was beautiful."[5]

While RIM executives laughed off the iPhone,[6] the second-generation device with 3G connectivity, GPS, and access to third-party apps via the Apple App Store was no joke. Effectively blindsided by the snowballing success of the iPhone, RIM did not have a comparable device in the pipeline. The inability of RIM's leaders to read customer desires in the wake of the iPhone left them unprepared to meet its market challenge. RIM could no longer claim product superiority in an area that it essentially created single-handedly. Before the iPhone, there was the BlackBerry. But before the BlackBerry, there was nothing. In the face of the now-obvious iPhone challenge, RIM rushed into smartphone development. Because of the initial inability of its senior management team to exercise the contextual competence to explore, RIM was forced into playing catch-up.

Apple's Steve Jobs was known for his contextual competence. He was very much the explorer throughout his career—from the early days of the Apple I geared to hobbyists, to the Apple II family of computers, to the Mac to the iPod, iPhone, and iPad. Peter Sims thought that Jobs's "unique genius was in his ability to foresee technology vectors and envision, design, and execute truly brilliant products and platforms."[7] In short, Jobs's contextual competence to explore allowed Apple to move forward.

Jobs is rightly credited for bringing user-friendly computers to the nontechnically inclined, as well as influencing and improving the computing experience for everyone. Not only that, Apple, thanks in large part to Jobs, has been able to sustain the brand: "Mac is the only personal computer with a 30-year history. Other than Apple itself, the leading computer companies of 1984 included names such as Atari, Commodore, Compaq, Kaypro and Radio Shack—all of which have since either left the PC business or vanished altogether. Even IBM... bailed on the PC industry in 2004. That the Mac has not only survived but thrived is astonishing."[8]

Before Apple was a household name, Jobs knew that computers did not have to be in the exclusive domain of large companies and university research labs. His revolutionary idea was that computers could be for everyone and not just for the techies who wanted to build and program their own boxes from scratch. Jobs had the ability to assess not only the climate of the computer industry but also the customer willingness to invest in computers for personal use. Digital anthropologist Frank Rose noted that "Steve Jobs proved ... that you can make technology personal and accessible, that you can combine form and function to create truly great products."[9] RIM's leadership typified the lack of contextual competence that led to its being stuck. Jobs was an example of the perpetual explorer as he continually attempted to create breakthrough products and ensure that Apple thought outside the box.

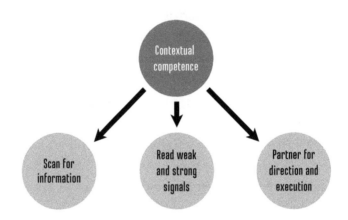

In exploring the context, pragmatic leaders have three challenges. First, they have to scan for information. That is, they have to analyze the sources of information. Second, they must read the signals. After scanning, they should be able to pick up and interpret both weak and strong signals indicating opportunities and hazards. Third, they must partner for exploration. Having networked and read the signals, they must connect with the key actors—especially stakeholders, constituents, and customers—to develop products and solutions that are aligned with the challenges, hazards, and opportunities that they pick up from reading the weak and strong signals.

## Scan for Information

Organizational leaders are bombarded by a massive amount of information. They are constantly caught in a deluge of data—some of it valuable, some of it less valuable, some of it worthless, and some that may be valuable down the road. Organizational leaders must take the time to actively analyze the data they come across. They must explore by scanning information sources to identify signals that suggest potential areas of innovation. George S. Day and Paul J.H. Schoemaker suggest that there are two types of scanning—passive scanning and active scanning. This section draws on their perspective as detailed in the volume *Peripheral Vision*.[10] Leaders who help their organizations break inertia can effectively balance both scanning methods.

### Passive Scanning

Passive scanning is the mundane, undirected, and largely automatic scanning of everyday information. Passive scanning implies the gathering of information from the usual sources, such as popular magazines or internal financial reports. Leaders "monitor key performance metrics and other indicators for assessing accountability, maintaining control, and guiding Six Sigma initiatives."[11] Passive scanning is undirected in the sense that the leaders may not be looking for anything specific or seeking an answer to an identifiable question. Almost on autopilot, leaders engaged in passive scanning comb through their usual sources of information as they look for anything out of the ordinary.

Leaders in myopic organizations, such as BlackBerry, primarily rely on passive scanning. They are consumed with analyzing information emanating from the same sources, which leads to enhanced focus yet predictable results. Passive scanning may bolster the sense that the organization is following and will not deviate from a pre-plotted direction. Day and Schoemaker observe, "Because most of the data comes from familiar, or traditional sources, this mode of scanning tends to reinforce, rather than challenge, prevailing beliefs."[12]

Passive scanning may allow leaders to spot opportunities and threats, albeit in an undirected and haphazard manner. In and of itself, passive scanning is not ideal for identifying and analyzing incoming signals. Simply put, the poor focus and lack of breadth of passive scanning makes it likely that valuable intelligence will be missed. Going back to BlackBerry, passive scanning contributed to the leadership decision that the company keep close to its knitting, which ultimately held them back.

**Active Scanning**

In contrast to passive scanning, active scanning can be either directed to address an explicit question or undirected with a wider and more ambiguous scope. While passive scanning is often haphazard, active scanning is deliberate, methodical, and forward looking. It tends to be "hypothesis driven."[13] Active scanning analyzes information from a wide variety of unorthodox sources, which may range from comments overheard on the street to Internet rants posted by dissatisfied customers. Day and Schoemaker weigh in again, "Active scanning reflects intense curiosity and emphasizes the further-out and fuzzier edges of the periphery."[14] Active scanning implies a continuous, active focus. Leaders who practice active scanning take the initiative to assemble teams that can troll various networks and comb through the seemingly disparate information to identify relevant signals.

It is particularly important to engage in active scanning in larger organizations, where "the scale and scope . . . creates problems of uncoordinated, distributed intelligence."[15] Active scanners need to develop the talent to uncover the information and insights that the organization's employees may have. A key to active scanning is not simply possessing bits of information, but having the cognitive discipline to understand its importance and relevance.

Another method of active scanning is to move outside of one's comfort zone. That is, diversify the content that one consumes every day. Active scanners often seek out new skills and use their newfound knowledge to inform their decision making. Or they may attend a conference or seminar in an adjacent field. Just having encounters and conversations with other professions may "spark new ideas."[16] More than one entrepreneur has discovered that developments in seemingly unrelated fields are connected and valuable.

The third method of active scanning is to tune in to what Day and Schoemaker call "the voice of the market."[17] Customers may use products in unconventional ways that can spur sales, such as repurposing skin-care lotion as bug repellent.[18] Leaders need to get their antennae out for the unexpected and unusual.

Active scanning of the market voice is improved through systematic analysis of specific client networks. Instead of looking at the behavior of every single customer, it is much more expedient to concentrate on the most important networks, such as complainers[19] and early adopters.[20] Complainers are those customers who do exactly that—they actively voice their critiques of the organization and/or its products and services. These customers may have purchased a defective product or had an entirely unsatisfactory sales experience. Complainers who offer pointed criticism can show leaders where their products or services are falling short.

Early adopters are the forward thinkers who immediately accept and purchase cutting-edge products. Early adopters eagerly purchase the newest technology not because of its novelty, but because of its inherent usefulness to their specialized needs. Early adopters offer organizational leaders a glimpse of what the future may hold for a specific product.

For an organization to break inertia, its leaders must succeed in balancing both passive and active scanning. On the one hand, they need to understand that they cannot rely on the constant analysis of routine information sources, which leads to a shallow understanding of the environment. On the other hand, too much active scanning may drill down too deeply, resulting in a lack of focus and direction, continuous reflection, hesitation, and organizational paralysis. Therefore, contextual competence depends not only on scanning but the ability to interpret signals, whether picked up actively or passively.

## Read Weak and Strong Signals

Martha Feldman and James March make the point that "organizations are consumers, managers, and purveyors of information."[21] Contextually competent leaders are explorers who can cut through environmental noise to read and manage both the weak and strong signals that emanate from all quarters. Not all information is immediately relevant and demands immediate action. Contextually competent leaders have developed the habit of being tuned to their environment and have acquired a sense of discernment. That is, they are not only able to detect what is going on, but they can prioritize what needs attention now, what needs more research, and what can be put on the back burner.

AM General Corporation first manufactured the High Mobility Multi-Purpose Wheeled Vehicle, popularly known as the Humvee or Hummer, as a military subcontractor in the 1980s. The brand was acquired by GM in 1998, but with production still headed by AM General, and the trucks were marketed to the civilian car-buying public. In the wake of the economic crisis of 2008, the future of the Hummer was in question. It developed a reputation for being a macho gas-guzzler. Unable to read the mounting signals that the public was more concerned with mileage as gas prices escalated, the brand suffered, and GM had to pull the plug on the Hummer in 2010.

As in the case of Hummer, a key component of reading signals is sense-making, which is the capacity to collect, order, and decipher information to inform the strategic intent and tactics of the organization.

Organizational theorist Karl Weick describes sense-making as a process of progressive clarification, "but this clarification often works in reverse."[22] That is, someone notices a condition or circumstance, and sense-making is the deliberate interpretation and speculation to the deeper meaning of the condition or circumstance. Leaders in thriving organizations accumulate pertinent information and decode its meaning. Through their networks, they pick up and make sense of the signals that others may regard as noise.

What is the essence of "making sense"? First, leaders receive the signals that ping from their environment and their networks, and then they digest and consider the implications of what the signals suggest. Contextually competent leaders are tuned to both weak and strong signals, giving them a grounded sense of what is going on around them. Signals suggest possible directions where the organization can move. The meaning of a strong signal is obvious and does not call for a biweekly committee meeting to mull it over. The implications of a strong signal are self-evident and leaders spend little time asking, "What does it mean?" Instead, they spend their time deciding whether to act, and what that action may be. For instance, a downswing in product demand by 32 percent at the height of the season indicates changing customer preferences and is a clear call to action. There may be different courses of action that organizational leaders can take in response, but the strength of this signal demands that organizational leaders make some decision. Similarly, if an organization launches a product that integrates key elements of existing products and has an amazing burst of sales, their success is a strong signal to competitors that they need to examine their product line right away. In both cases, strong signals demand a reaction. Even if leaders ultimately do nothing, that nondecision is reached consciously, and is a direct reaction to the relevant information that the leaders learn.

Weak signals are indirect and ambiguous, with no clear reactive course of action. While strong signals are easily monitored, read, and acted on, weak signals sometimes take a longer lead to action because leaders need the time to decipher, deliberate, and discuss. A strong signal elicits a question: What needs to be done? The weak signal asks, What does this mean?

A weak signal offers grounds for hunches and speculation. The potential reaction—or range of reactions—that a weak signal prompts is not obvious. Think of weak signals as shadows that need to be interpreted for the edges to be sharpened and for the surface to come into view. Weak signals exist at "the blurry zone at the edge of an organization's vision"[23] and require leaders not simply to have their antenna out, but to research deeply the ramifications of any course of action. Weak signals are flickering, inconsistent, and volatile. Weak signals can be fragmented and unclear, and easily dismissed as static until they are interpreted. Weak signals are like breadcrumbs scattered on a path—irregular with missing data, but leading somewhere. With careful discernment, the value of the assorted bits of information becomes apparent and the organization can convert the breadcrumbs into a giant leap forward.

Persistent weak signals can be a harbinger of a direct signal—and can give a leader an indication that forethought and adaptation are necessary. If a direct signal develops unexpectedly and on short notice, the leader may not be able to make necessary adjustments to prevent hitting the iceberg ahead. Leaders in thriving organizations are sensitized to weak signals, which can help them stay ahead of the game. They make it a practice not only to sense trends, but to think seriously about the trends and what the implications are for their organization.

Contextually competent leaders identify strengthening signals and review the range of alternative responses. They try to understand the context and explore it in depth. At the same time, they are also tuned to stronger signals. Consider the general public's increasing awareness of and interest in the benefits of healthy eating and engaging in a healthy lifestyle. Leaders in different industries have reacted to this overall trend with distinct responses.

PepsiCo had been stuck for years: "Sales of carbonated soft drinks have dropped 14% over nine years, and Pepsi's market share has fallen too. The company has struggled just to keep its revenues and profits essentially frozen in place."[24] Faced with discouraging numbers, the CEO of PepsiCo, Indra Nooyi, had to react and lead. Not only were the numbers poor, but nutrition experts, politicians, and media commentators openly criticized the company's line of prototypical junk food. Nooyi knew that a steady diet of potato chips and cola drinks, Pepsi's main sources of revenue, was detrimental to the overall health of customers.[25] What's more, she saw that her customers knew this too. Nooyi recognized that young consumers had a growing interest in healthier eating.

In response, PepsiCo began a rebranding effort, sorting their products into three categories.[26] While chips and soda are "fun for you" foods, Pepsi started to offer "good for you" products made from oatmeal and "better for you" snacks (like baked chips).[27] She worked to ensure that all products, including "fun for you" snacks, would be healthier than their predecessors. PepsiCo made a clear shift and showed that they were working in the interests of the customer.

By 2015, PepsiCo was showing signs of a "real comeback,"[28] and the stock price was rebounding. Nooyi read the strong signals in sales indicating that customers' health concerns were influencing their eating habits and recognized that a reliance on PepsiCo's old line of products would not allow the organization to thrive. PepsiCo was willing to diversify their snack-food offerings by offering healthier choices. Because its leaders could read signals, PepsiCo was poised to give consumers the healthier products they desired.

Another company that picked up the health-consciousness vibe is

Fitbit. Fitbit virtually created the wearable fitness-tracking market. The clip-on device with an internal motion detector found fans among all kinds of sports enthusiasts. The gadget was not only a serious tool for the professional athlete but also an affordable novelty for the casual user whose fitness aspiration was to count steps. Information about activity could be wirelessly transmitted to allow users to check their heart rate, monitor calories burned, log food consumption, and track sleep patterns.[29] Fitbit's genius was that its founders James Park and Eric Friedman saw a way to marry consumer interest in knowing their personal stats with the available technology. Fitbit skillfully read the signs—they saw the potential of wearable technology and the burgeoning trend toward health consciousness and wholesome living. Combining the two, they carved out a new place in the market to thrive. Since then, newer generations of Fitbit can be linked to a variety of smartphones, and tech giants like Google, Apple, and Samsung are also looking for opportunities in this space.[30]

In 1998, Vancouver-based Lululemon created a line of comfortable clothing for the yoga enthusiast. Founder Chip Wilson had just sold Westbeach, a surf, skate, and snowboard lifestyle company when he took up yoga. He noticed that in yoga classes, "the women were wearing bulky cotton shirts and shorts and I knew I could do better. I also knew that yoga, with its intense relaxing effects, was going to be really big."[31] His prognostication proved to be right: "The number of US yoga practitioners has increased to more than 36 million, up from 20.4 million in 2012, while annual practitioner spending on yoga classes, clothing, equipment, and accessories rose to $16 billion, up from $10 billion over the past four years."[32]

It wasn't just the clothing in sustainable, breathable fabrics that Lululemon was selling, it was a lifestyle: "The stores offer an array of men's and women's athletic wear, yoga mats and informational books and videos about yoga and natural healing—everything the yoga practitioner needs to get on the path to enlightenment."[33] Lululemon's founder, by exploring in the environment of his own hobby, picked up the weak signals emitting around him and created market opportunity. He saw the immense potential and gaining popularity of yoga, as well as the wholesome lifestyle it is associated with. He realized that yoga wear, as well as clothing for other athletic pursuits, would be something that health-conscious consumers were willing to buy.

These examples show how different industries leveraged the signals for increasing interest in health consciousness. PepsiCo's core products were soda and snacks, but company leaders realized that it would need to introduce a healthier range of products to stay competitive. The success of Fitbit shows how a fitness trend could be used to build a new wearable technology device. Meanwhile, Lululemon saw the signs that yoga would be the next big fitness trend, and it is continuing to attract practitioners of all ages. The leaders of Lululemon and Fitbit read and reacted to the weak signals of health-conscious consumers and led their respective companies into new markets before their competitors, whereas PepsiCo's Indra Nooyi interpreted the strong signal of stagnating profits and decreasing market share as a pointed suggestion to adjust her product line.

Strong signals can be weak signals that have matured and gained strength, such as emerging technology that quickly gains traction or a practice that was considered outrageous in the recent past but has evolved into a best practice. Strong signals clearly point to industry developments and strategies of competitors.

To a certain degree, market laggers are more likely to act on strong signals than weak ones. Market laggers, for numerous and legitimate reasons, may be hesitant to pursue an identified weak signal. They may not take the initiative and react immediately. Their leaders may have some awareness of a growing signal forecasting a possible direction or trend, but they deem the risk, hassle, and bother of an investment not worth the effort and too much of a deviation from their core activities. However, once a weak signal gains traction and is an undeniable trend, market laggers may be stimulated into action, making the appropriate adjustments or committing the necessary resources.

As a counterpoint to Lululemon and the ability of its leaders to read the weak signals of the yoga industry, as late as 2014, Mickey Drexler, CEO of J. Crew Group, declared, "We don't have the expertise to do that,"—"that" being activewear.[34] Late to the party, J. Crew finally launched a line of stylish yet functional fitness gear for both men and women in 2017. While J. Crew did not pick up and react to the weak signals as readily as some of their competitors—who already made deep inroads in this market—they read and reacted to the strong signals with a cautious approach that wouldn't endanger their brand. Today they are in the activewear game, and in a very visible way.

Signals are interesting in that an organization can have the wherewithal to pick up weak signals, and in the process, by finding success in a specific market or niche, can become the source of a strong signal for a competitor. In the wake of the Napster debacle, the rising tide of the popularity of MP3s was a weak signal that the crumbling music industry refused to hear.

Apple realized that CDs were dead and that file sharing was the wave of the future. The challenge was to make file sharing not only legal but also profitable. In 2003, iTunes was launched. Essentially, iTunes provided a legal method to buy and sell online music tied directly to the iPod.[35] Steve Jobs wisely presented iTunes as a win-win for both Apple and the music industry. He predicted that the former would profit from the sale of its iPod hardware, while the latter would do the same from the legal online distribution of its music. Initially, Jobs had difficulty convincing the leaders of the major labels to join iTunes. Negotiations were tense, and many correctly argued that Apple was getting the better end of the deal. However, by its 2003 launch, the five key players—Universal, EMI, Warner, Sony, and BMG—had agreed to sign with iTunes.[36]

iTunes was a hit: "One million songs were downloaded in the store's first week, 25 million by the end of 2003, and one billion by February of 2006. iPod sales responded in kind, jumping from under one million in 2003 to over four million in 2004 to a staggering 22.5 million in 2005."[37] The success of iTunes was a strong signal that legal online downloads were the future of the music industry. The record labels read this strong signal, and in the following months agreed to sign and renew their iTunes contracts into the foreseeable future.

Another weak-to-strong signal was Nintendo's early success in bringing about the portable gaming revolution and the subsequent attempts of its competitors to emulate it. Before Nintendo, portable gaming was a dream. Having the ability to play a game on the go was in the realm of science fiction—something that could be achieved only in the far-off future. This changed with Nintendo's 1980s release of the Game & Watch, which was a "game . . . package[d] . . . in a small box with a screen and some buttons."[38] Unlike today's portable gaming consoles, the Game & Watch could only play one rudimentary game. As such, its appeal was limited. However, Nintendo sold multiple versions of Game & Watch, each with its own LCD game. The product won mass-market appeal, and soon sales amounted to 43.4 million units.[39]

In the 1990s Nintendo took handheld gaming to the next level with the Game Boy. The device allowed players to switch games using the same box. Nintendo developed dozens of diverse and now classic games for the platform, which could be played as soon as the game cartridge was clicked into place. Game Boy was a runaway success, sending a clear strong signal that portable gaming was commercially viable. Nintendo "ignite[d] the handheld console to such a degree that, in less than a decade, 64.42 million Game Boy units were in the hands of gamers globally."[40]

Nintendo's competitors read the strong signal of its success and responded by launching their own portable gaming devices. The early 2000s saw a flurry of new entrants into this industry. In 2003, Nokia launched the N-Gage, a smartphone with 3D graphics designed specifically to play video games. In 2005, Sony's PlayStation Portable was released. Sony Computer president and CEO Ken Kutaragi dubbed the device "the Walkman of the 21st century."[41] Seeing where Nintendo was in the market inspired its rivals to follow suit.

Whether they are market leaders or market laggers, thriving organizations have leaders who are constantly aware of the environment. Clunky and myopic organizations read signals, but they have developed some peculiar traits when reading signals that make it difficult for them to truly thrive.

Leaders in clunky organizations find it difficult to maintain a common focus. With each division or product line pursuing its own interest, any exploration and interpretation of the environmental cues happens at the unit level (if it happens at all)—impeding the firm's ability to put together a unified, company-wide response. Similarly, the blinder mind-set of myopic organizations makes it difficult for leaders to objectively pick up external signals that could suggest a modification of its core product or a natural expansion of its customer base. Clunkiness, with its turf-like characteristics, may lead to prolonged debate and even conflict over the interpretation of signals, while myopia may lead to a rationalization of any interpretation in the context of the status quo. Leaders in both clunky and myopic organizations could easily fail as explorers if they are unable to respond to and align the organization to the external context. To do this, they may need to create partnerships.

## Partner for Direction and Execution

Having recognized the environmental signals, contextually competent leaders often partner with key parties to define the essence and implications of these signals, trends, and patterns they've picked up. In trying to deepen their sense-making and further understand the implications of the cues they've detected, pragmatic leaders establish deep partnerships with key parties. These partnerships, based on the sharing and exchange of information and continuous dialogue, help them translate the signals into concrete ideas, specific actions, and new policies. Such a partnership not only enhances the leader's capacity to make sense of signals but also enhances the capacity to respond to signals in a specific and relevant fashion. In trying to flesh out the specific implications of signals, contextually competent explorers partner for direction and execution. These partnerships, through active exchange and dialogue, reduce the possibility of misinterpretation of trends and signals and increase the probability of an appropriate response.

### Partner for Direction

Contextually competent leaders seek out others to help them see what is ahead—not just next week, but next year and ten years down the road. Organizations that break inertia partner for direction primarily through their efforts to team up with customers. Customers are ready-made allies, supporters, and, increasingly, "co-creators of value."[42] Netflix's leaders actively partner with customers. Most of the time, Netflix reads the signals correctly, but sometimes they miss the mark. Partnering with their customers can be a confirmation that they read the signals correctly. In this context, the company takes pride in its ability to remain flexible and respond to customer feedback, such as the disastrous moment when the leaders decided to break up the service into two separate systems: streaming and DVD delivery. The backlash was immediate and customers made it known quite emphatically that they were not fans.

In a blog post for customers, Netflix CEO Reed Hastings admitted: "It is clear that for many of our members two websites would make things more difficult, so we are going to keep Netflix as one place to go for streaming and DVDs. . . . This means no change: one website, one account, one password . . . in other words, no Qwikster."[43]

For Netflix, it made perfect sense to divide the business, but they didn't think it through from the customer's perspective. In a public apology issued via the *New York Times*, Hastings recalled, "I realized, if our business is about making people happy, which it is, then I had made a mistake."[44] By taking the initiative to partner with customers and respond to customer feedback, Netflix improved operational integration. Netflix enhanced its position as an industry leader by learning to respond to customers.

Leaders in organizations that break inertia don't simply focus on selling products or generating short-term fixes, but emphasize customer relationships as strategic partnerships. They help their clients envision the future of their business, even if this vision does not serve the short-term intent of selling available products or providing immediate solutions. Establishing this type of relationship provides the essential deep information that may be frustrating in the short term, but may point to critical directions in the longer term.

Deutsche Post DHL Group (DHL) is the world's largest postal and international courier service company. Under the leadership of CEO Frank Appel, innovation is a strategic imperative: "As pioneers in logistics we make a decisive contribution to shaping the future of this industry."[45] DHL has achieved its innovations to lead in the industry in part by partnering with its customers.

DHL's leaders actively involve its customers in the process of creating and testing new technology through customer innovation and trend workshops in Germany. In the workshops, DHL works with customers to develop new products, services, and processes and to identify logistics trends. There have been over six thousand engagements with customers. DHL is leveraging the customer to gain insights into possible future trends. Products that were inspired by the workshops include the parcelcopter, a drone that transports goods, and an augmented reality platform enabled by smart glasses to improve warehousing operations. These workshops allow customers not only to share their perspectives but also to learn about the challenges DHL faces as a global logistics company.

Long-term relationships are costly to cultivate, but the potential payoff is more than worth it. In 2015, DHL dedicated $10 million to build an innovation center in Singapore to increase understanding of the Asian market. In July 2017, DHL announced plans to open a similar innovation center in the United States. The results of DHL's customer engagement speak for themselves. Customer satisfaction is over 80 percent. On-time delivery performance is 97 percent. Customer churn rates decreased. The takeaway is that "DHL discovered . . . its customers wanted to help in rethinking their supply chains to improve business performance."[46] Appel has transformed customer relationships into strategic partnerships, and now DHL is well positioned to see the future of logistics.

Netflix CEO Reed Hastings cares about partnering with customers to give them a better video-viewing service. Netflix is on top of customer trends. Communications director Jonathan Friedland says, "We know what people watch on Netflix and we're able with a high degree of confidence to understand how big a likely audience is for a given show based on people's viewing habits."[47] Partnering with customers enables the company to use customer data to not only enhance the creation of programming but also to fine-tune its "binge-release strategy" where an entire season is launched at the same time.[48] Customer data also feeds the recommendation algorithm, where the service will suggest what to view next.[49] Netflix partners with customers to improve and enhance their viewing experience.

Leaders in thriving organizations need to let their clients know that they are willing to take on a short-term loss for the potential of a long-term gain. In short, they must make it clear that their organizations will value customer relationships over immediate gains. Thriving organizations will prototype a concept at cost or invest time for a new program without a guarantee of return. Their leaders view the initial cost of gaining traction with customers as a worthy investment. In the words of Southwest's Herb Kelleher: "We were going to enable more people to fly. It didn't matter whether we had competition or not. In other words, we just said we're a different type of cat. When we get a load factor that gets into the 70 or 75 percent range over an appreciable period of time, we don't increase fares. We add flights and put additional seats in. So if you come from that basic position, that this is what you are, then of course you have to have low costs."[50]

That said, contextually competent leaders know that too much client alignment can backfire. They understand the importance of balancing partner (i.e., customer, client, supplier, etc.) alignment with the firm's overall corporate-level strategy. To break inertia, leaders have to be willing to make adjustments for their partners, but at the same time ensure that they do not let the needs of specific partners jeopardize the organization's strategic business intent.

**Partner for Execution**

Environmental signals and trends may demand that pragmatic leaders partner not only to define a new direction, but also for execution. Signals and trends may indicate a need to implement a new direction or strategy, which may be essential to breaking inertia and avoiding sluggishness. That said, pragmatic leaders understand that in pursuing a different direction, they may not be able to do it alone. They may need to partner with others to delineate the execution and share expertise, talent, and even resources. As such, signals and trends may lead contextually competent leaders to become aware of the necessity of partnering with the leaders of other organizations—even competitors—to execute. The apparent losses that an organization may incur by entering a partnership are often outweighed by the rewards of working together. In partnering for execution, "it is crucial to balance the interests and backgrounds of the partners . . . so that a win-win situation is created."[51] Partners need to deliberately "manage the delicate balance between competition and cooperation."[52]

Motorola chairman Bob Galvin, the son of the company's founder, sought to improve his company's opportunities after facing fierce competition in semiconductors in the 1980s. His plan was to enter the Japanese market through a partnership to increase revenue in a space other US firms had failed to thrive in. The partner was Toshiba, a top-tier Japanese technology firm and a direct competitor of Motorola's. Toshiba was falling behind in the microprocessor arena and saw an opportunity to assume leadership in microprocessors with Motorola. Motorola was the third-largest semiconductor company in the world at the time and the leader in microprocessors. Motorola was willing to share its technology with Toshiba. In return, Motorola would leverage Toshiba's distribution channels and manufacturing expertise to penetrate the Japanese market. At the time, Motorola's executive vice president Stephen Levy said that "gaining access to the Japanese market has been a very slow process. This partnership with Toshiba will enable us to accelerate our efforts to service this important market."[53]

The partnership did not start smoothly. Many analysts and Motorola employees feared that Toshiba would, over time, learn Motorola's design secrets and compete directly using their superior manufacturing technology. One observer noted, "Early on in the Toshiba-Motorola alliance, engineers were reluctant to share semiconductor production technology with people who just months before had been their competitors."[54] Motorola senior management reinforced to managers and employees at all levels that the partnership was mutually beneficial.

To this day, the Motorola-Toshiba alliance is a successful partnership amid complicated trade laws and proprietary technology. Motorola's market share increased and, with a larger presence in Japan, won a contract with the Japanese government in 1990 to use their technology as the standard for mobile phones. The partnership allowed Toshiba to establish itself as the number one producer of microchips in the world. Motorola and Toshiba continue to identify new opportunities to better compete by partnering together in the ever-changing technology space. In 2014, Toshiba partnered with Motorola to resell their products through Toshiba's global retail distribution, in return for access to Motorola's portfolio of innovative solutions.

A leader who understands when to partner with a competitor is Netflix CEO Reed Hastings. He led Netflix's partnership with Amazon Web Services (AWS). AWS is a cloud-computing platform and provides data storage.[55] Netflix's core is in video-streaming content, and Amazon directly competes with Netflix through its Prime Video services. However, both organizations ultimately benefit from working with the other. Hastings argued that what "increasing competition in the Internet TV arena does is make people more able and willing to cut the cord of so-called 'linear' or traditional cable TV."[56]

Hastings's decision to shift all website, data, and streaming services to AWS was driven by a major database corruption in 2008 and a major data-center fire in 2010. AWS offered Netflix "the greatest ability to scale—something which was critical for a business growing at their pace—but also the greatest portfolio of services."[57] The move allowed

Netflix to focus on their core service, video-streaming content, and to better deliver to customers. Netflix also provided AWS with legitimacy as a resource for large Internet companies. While it may seem odd for Amazon to be helping Netflix better compete against them, AWS provides significant revenue for Bezos to reinvest into growing his company and Netflix is one of AWS's biggest clients. The two leaders have found a relationship to succeed together.

Frequently, organizational leaders overcome inertia by combining resources and working together to discover new possibilities and execute effectively. Instead of solely relying on their own resources, leaders of both organizations know when to share resources to better partner with external stakeholders like customers, suppliers, or other organizations, to their mutual benefit.

Apple Pay is the contactless payment service launched by Apple in 2014, and the service now accounts for almost three-quarters of the contactless payments made in the United States.[58]

> Apple Pay . . . let[s] shoppers load their credit card and debit card information onto iPhones' "mobile wallets." Customers can then use either their iPhone (or linked Apple Watch) to pay at retail stores equipped with point-of-sale registers supporting near-field communication (NFC) technology, which enables frictionless payments between smartphones and registers. People simply place their phones or watches near the point-of-sale register sensors for a payment to be made without swiping a card.[59]

Introducing the app with such large players like MasterCard and Visa gives Apple the chance to work out potential problems while new issuing banks and retailers ramp up their ability to accept and process the cards. MasterCard has a strong commitment to Apple

Pay, as shown by the launch of MasterCard Nearby that allows users to find locations where Apple Pay is accepted,[60] and its development of the Master Card Digital Enablement System (MDES) that enables the secure tokenization of cardholder data.[61]

Apple Pay continues to be successful not only because of the security, privacy, and user-friendliness of the transactions, but also because of the partnerships that Apple forged within the financial services sector. As a leader of a thriving organization, Tim Cook understands the importance of these partnerships for the execution of Apple Pay.

Such technical execution can occur in partnerships between competitors, building on the strengths and possibilities of both organizations. This way, rivals stay thriving. An outstanding competitor partnership is between IBM and Apple to develop and integrate "the iOS platform into enterprise mobility."[62] The venture, which provides a suite of tools that can be used in various industries, has been successful: "The apps have been designed by combining IBM's big data and analytics capabilities with Apple's customer centric business model to help companies achieve new levels of efficiency, effectiveness and customer satisfaction out of the box. This includes the integration of Watson's cognitive capabilities into the apps so they can continuously learn about the users by building on the data they collect."[63]

Contextually competent leaders like Apple's Tim Cook show no hesitation to reach out beyond their immediate expertise to find partners. Apple brings a lot to the table. Its products are integrated into the daily life of many people around the world and its partners have similar brand profiles. Working together, they can make each other better.

▲  ▲  ▲

Pragmatic organizational leaders need to figure out what's happening around them and where they're going. What are the new directions and trends suggested by the market? What is the potential for innovation? These questions need to be answered to break inertia and ensure that the organization will thrive and move ahead. Organizations need leaders who have the pragmatic skills to be contextually aware and capable of exploring their environment, reading both weak and strong signals, deciphering trends, picking up cues, and making sense of what's happening around them. Armed with such information, contextually competent leaders partner with key actors and organizations to deepen their understanding of their initial interpretation. They partner with others to plot new directions and, when possible, to collaborate on execution. In the world of rapidly changing technology, shifting politics, fads and foibles, and multigenerational diversity of taste, understanding the changing context under which the organization operates is critical to getting out of the doldrums of inertia.

## FACILITATE IDEATION

Pragmatic organizational leaders may achieve contextual competence by exploring their environment, reading cues, and sensing the current and future direction of business. They may be on top of subtle trends, grasp the disposition of changing markets, and detect indications of advances in tech. Because of their exploratory capacity, they are able to help their organization be aware of industry opportunity, customer needs, and future directions. That said, this is only the first step in leading for robust discovery.

Organizations may have leaders who are totally capable of exploring their environment, yet fail to take the spark of an idea and implant it within an organization in such a way that it results in real action, specific innovation, and lasting change. For discovery to occur, pragmatic leaders must create the organizational environment in which ideas can be freely discussed and shared and provide the psychosocial space where those ideas can move from abstraction and insight into actual change and innovation. They must have ideational competence. They must be concrete innovators. They must be proficient in moving beyond an initial idea and pushing it into the realm of reality. Ideationally competent leaders ensure that both weak and strong signals are not dismissed due to the stagnation of clunky or myopic-induced organizational inertia.

Organizations with myopic tendencies may have leaders who can read the signals in their environment and understand what is happening around them. However, in a myopic setting, these leaders, as tuned in as they may be, may fail to move their organizations beyond the blinder mind-set, resulting in minimal or no innovation. RadioShack and Kodak were cognizant of the trends but lagged on the innovation curve. Like leaders in organizations with myopic tendencies, leaders in organizations with clunky tendencies may notice and interpret signals. However, because of the loose structures and unintegrated business strategy of clunky firms, it may become difficult for these leaders to create the synergy necessary to convert initial insights into innovation.

A myopic organization may continue doing what it's always done despite exploration. Any innovation that occurs will be safe, occasional, and incremental. Conversely, clunky organizations may have many ideas rattling around, but few will emerge as a viable prototype. Without leaders who have ideational competence to move ideas and innovations, good insights based on sound intelligence will result in nothing.

To ensure discovery, pragmatic leaders need to create the group synergy necessary for ideation. They cannot assume that the synergy necessary for significant ideation will occur without their direct involvement. Ideationally competent leaders enhance this critical group

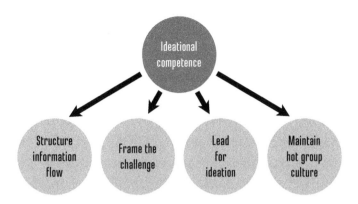

synergy by making sure that information flows freely, leading their teams in framing the innovation challenge, and creating the environment for collective ideation. Finally, these leaders must help maintain a hot group culture, which permits team members to coalesce around and get excited by new ideas and new directions, unhampered by hierarchies, structures, and inertia. These four core elements of ideational competence allow the ideation process to move toward concrete results and ensure that the organization breaks inertia.

## Structure Information Flow

Turf and complexity are obstacles that clunky organizations need to overcome when moving innovation. Each unit may have its own version of tunnel vision, which makes collaboration extremely difficult. A free flow of information is crucial to breaking inertia. Information sharing covers a range of activities from one-on-one encounters, "departmental meetings, written reports, telephone conversations, [and] water-cooler meetings. . . . It seems that sharing occurs uniquely with information, in ways not replicated with other goods and services."[64]

Ideationally competent leaders foster information flow to reinforce a sense of collective purpose to promote cross-organizational integration and collaboration.

Tesla puts a premium on information sharing. Chief designer Franz von Holzhausen says that the firm's information-sharing practices allow it to "move incredibly fast."[65] The power of enhanced information sharing is evidenced by the development of the Tesla S. Von Holzhausen's team was "just three designers sitting next to their engineering counterparts,"[66] which allowed for free and constant interaction.

Incomplete information sharing and the lack of continuous dialogue can impede innovation. Indeed, this barrier to innovation can be removed only by fostering information flow, which can be brought about by encouraging a sense of a collective purpose, reducing hierarchies, and minimizing turf struggles.

Apple consistently overcomes inertia because its leadership nurtures an integrated collective to improve information flow. After returning to Apple in 1997, Jobs found that the company's organizational structure had become a barrier to innovation. At the time, Apple had sixteen different divisions and sixteen marketing budgets. Some may say there were sixteen fiefdoms, which meant operational delays and the restriction of information flow. Apple had become clunky, with each division operating in pursuit of its individual vision.

Jobs knew that each unit was critical to Apple's success. As such, he understood that the success of his innovation agenda was dependent on his ability to build the cross-organizational support that allowed for the rapid flow of information. Consequently, he consolidated Apple's sixteen marketing budgets into one that he controlled: "There would be one advertising budget; divisions would compete for ad dollars."[67] This budget consolidation created an environment that forced collaboration and the flow of information. Division leaders could no longer work solely in their own bubbles—they now had to cooperate across the organization and share information efficiently to make effective use of the sole budget. They now had to collaborate, share information, and support Jobs's singular innovation agenda instead of working on their pet projects while ensconced in their individual spheres. If they did not cooperate with the wider organization, they could not expect support from others when it came time to market their products. As an innovator, Jobs restructured the organization to enhance information flow.

While restructuring can enhance information flow, Lou Gerstner understood that without a sense of collective purpose, any simple restructuring would be ineffective.[68] In the 1990s, IBM was a classic clunky organization weighed down by decentralization, autonomous departments and divisions, stagnant information flow, and constant internal strife. Gerstner remarked, "Units competed with each other, hid things from each other. Huge staffs spent countless hours debating and managing transfer pricing terms between IBM units instead of facilitating a seamless transfer of products to customers."[69] To break inertia, he knew that IBM had to achieve some integration and a sense of the collective to allow for fluid flow of information and ideas.

In 1993, after becoming IBM's CEO, he decided that the company had to integrate its operations to improve information flow and its innovation capacity. Gerstner recalls, "We needed to integrate as a team inside the company so that we could integrate for the customers on their premises."[70] Demonstrating the importance of operational integration, the CEO "famously put the brakes on a plan, which was already well under way, to break up the company into several operating units."[71] He knew that internal conflict would escalate with more groups, and that effective integration could help foster collaboration and improve communication. Gerstner further emphasized integration by consolidating the company's various advertising agencies. Understanding the importance of a unified marketing plan, he clearly saw the confusion created by IBM's mixed messaging. From now on, only one voice would sell the IBM brand.[72] Gerstner understood that conveying organizational unity externally was not enough. There had to be a sense of collective purpose from within as well to get employees to communicate better. Gerstner launched a series of initiatives to foster the creation of a culture to back his integration strategy. One was that "every employee would make three 'personal business commitments,' or actions to fulfill broader IBM commitments. Performance against those commitments was directly tied to salary."[73] By instituting yearly commitments, Gerstner emphasized the importance of collective effort and laid the groundwork for the creation of a strong culture of teamwork.

Gerstner's second initiative for unity and collaboration was the creation of a new compensation system that tied individual pay to overall corporate performance—employees were rewarded for delivering on shared organizational goals. Early on, Gerstner had found this new system to be a necessity, especially for IBM's executives. Aside from their tendency to compete against one another more fiercely than against their external competition, IBM's executives viewed their roles as being largely ceremonious. One observer noted that the norm was that "senior executives at IBM were expected to preside, to review. They didn't do the work."[74] The thinking was that if their paychecks were at stake, executives would feel less entitled, and would feel a greater need to contribute to the collective purpose and deliver results. With less hierarchy, employees across the organization could feel safer in their interactions with higher-ups, which would lead to improvements in communication and information flow to advance the organizational agenda.

Through unit consolidation and tying individual rewards to

collective achievement, Gerstner, as an innovator, transformed IBM into an integrated entity in which collaboration, cooperation, and information sharing was not only possible but also necessary for individual success. Gerstner, as much as he could, strove to steer IBM away from its clunky tendency and toward a more structurally integrated organization in which all actors were incentivized to work within the context of the collective. He lessened internal competition and strife and freed information flow from the weight of bureaucracy. The consequence was that IBM became a bit less clunky and a bit more agile, capable of making adjustments in response to shifting environmental signals.

In a clunky setting, such as IBM, information flow may be hampered because of the lack of structural integration. In a myopic organization, the information flow may be hindered disproportionately by the focused mind-set, which can result in key actors ignoring, rationalizing, or delaying action on available information. The often unstated and sometimes dysfunctional philosophy held by many in a myopic setting is "It worked in the past, it's working now, let's not upset the apple cart. Let's play it safe, we know who we are, we know what we are about." In the context of the myopic tendency, if inertia is to be broken, pragmatic leaders must put a special emphasis on creating processes that allow and encourage individuals to promote new ideas and push boundaries with a deep sense of psychological safety.

When Mark King became the CEO of Adidas in 2014, he worked to build a new culture of innovation.[75] King wanted to encourage innovation from all corners of the company and eliminate its clunky and myopic tendencies. He promoted safety and inclusion in his efforts to improve creative information flow. One of the ways he did this was by creating the Adidas Group Innovation Academy (aGIA), an online training platform.[76] To complete the training, participants had to come up with "one big idea for the brand."[77] Over a thousand ideas were slashed to "100 ideas under a dozen different themes."[78] Ultimately, one idea would be funded.

One Adidas innovation manager attributed aGIA's success to its "elements of meritocracy."[79] Hierarchy and status are eliminated on the online learning platform, with no mention of job title, empowering individuals to feel safe to promote their viewpoints and ideas. Participants are known in the online community by "only their name, their photo and a reflection of their contribution to the community by way of an 'innovator score.'"[80] The more employees contribute, the higher their score, actively rewarding creativity without demanding participation. Employees from across the organization become integrated into a culture of collaboration and creation. They become enthusiastic individuals engaged in a collective purpose, promoting the free flow of creative information needed to avoid the blinder mind-set.

## Frame the Challenge

While enhancing information flow is essential to creating synergy necessary for ideation, pragmatic leaders know that framing the challenge—defining the parameters of any change or innovation initiative—is equally important. Pragmatic leaders know that there is tension between framing a challenge too broadly or too narrowly. To break inertia and ensure ideation, leaders must understand the pitfalls of going too far in either direction. Leading for ideation implies having the responsibility of framing the organizational challenge and making clear to others the size of the canvas that is available to work with. Is the organizational group restricted to the small canvas focusing primarily on short-term goals, or are the challenges broad and far reaching, demanding a larger canvas? The scope of service, definition of the problem, nature of production, number of resources, and availability of time are among the factors that may affect the size of the innovation canvas. Ideationally competent leaders are keenly aware of the implications of framing organizational challenges using each or both canvases.

## Working with a Small Canvas

Leaders who choose to work with a smaller, tighter canvas operate under many constraints and a defined direction. They define the goal and intentions of the project clearly. With a tight canvas, there is a routinized search process. That is, for every problem and challenge that presents itself, it is clear how to diagnose it. It usually involves innovating with the intent to satisfy customers' defined needs or to develop specific products or services.

A smaller canvas may be useful in tackling short-term challenges. The short term implies having less available time, dealing with common problems, approaching things in an incremental manner, and having a narrower scope. By initially limiting the extent of possible divergence, leaders framing the challenge with a smaller canvas focus the direction of their innovation team. Instead of having to spend their collective time chasing down every possible lead, team members can concentrate on following up on a few. As such, the group can quickly achieve the innovation it seeks.

The Sony Walkman pioneered portable music. Sony's innovation wasn't to create a breakthrough product from scratch, but to tinker with an existing product. The company had a cassette recorder on the market whose primary function was to record audio with a playback function. Sony's cofounder and honorary chairman Masaru Ibuka used this bulky machine to listen to music while he traveled, and he "instructed the tape recorder division to create a smaller version for his personal use."[81] To build the Walkman, Sony's engineers did not make something new, but removed features from the cassette recorder to make a smaller device for the music fan.

In building the Walkman, Sony leaders adopted a small canvas. They had a specific goal: to use the skills of their engineers to miniaturize electronics and remodel an existing product to create a gadget that revolutionized portable music. Adopting a small canvas also increased the speed of delivery. It took just four months (with encouragement from Sony chairman Akio Morita) to transform the prototype into a marketable, affordable, and profitable consumer product.[82]

As the Sony example shows, a small canvas implies a clearly defined goal. Innovations produced using a small canvas are often incremental and product focused. This does not mean that the canvas cannot be stretched to create game-changing, dramatic innovation. The late 1980s launch of the NEC Ultralite computer shows how a leader can adapt and stretch the canvas to create revolutionary products: "In the late 1980s an engineering team at NEC devising a way to program business telephones developed an unusually small computer terminal. When vice president Tom Martin saw how lightweight it was, he asked if it could be made to run MS-DOS. When the engineers said that would be easy, he realized he had the makings of something big—a new kind of portable PC—and he quickly assembled a cross-functional team to develop it."[83]

Initially working with a small canvas, NEC's engineering team attempted to improve business telephones. As the team moved forward, innovation excitement struck Martin. He had a hunch that the tiny computer terminal could lead to a breakthrough. He had a vision of an extremely lightweight, portable PC—something unheard of. Martin stretched the innovation canvas and ventured into unknown territory but with a clear destination in mind. He allowed for a greater amount of divergent thinking, and loosened time and resource availability to get to a clearly defined result: making the computer terminal run MS-DOS and creating a consumer-friendly product.

The Ultralite PC, one of the first true laptops, was born. Its small-scale size gave rise to the term "notebook" to distinguish it from the much larger laptops. "At just over four pounds, the laptop was under half the weight of its nearest competitor, and its backlit screen was a technical marvel."[84] To this day, the Ultralite is regarded as a landmark technological breakthrough in mobile computing.

## Working with a Large Canvas

Whereas a small canvas is narrow and specific, allowing for quick progress toward a well-defined goal, a larger canvas allows for abundant creativity. When leaders frame the challenge with a large canvas, they allow an organization to step into new territory, leading to fresh directions and long-term focused changes that can be essential for it to thrive. Larger canvases often consider problems and solutions of a more undefined nature rather than with the nuts-and-bolts of specific products. Although the result may be the creation of a radical product, these innovations are rooted in the search to find a solution to a problem.

Apple brought the computer to the larger public. Netflix made entertainment accessible on demand. Amazon changed the face of shopping. At the outset, each of these organizations asked how they could solve a business problem. They did not set out to produce a groundbreaking product or service, but they bravely dove into once-unfamiliar terrain and disrupted the status quo. In the case of Apple, the organization sought to answer a question: How can we bring the computer from the realm of professional tech users to everyone? Although there was a clear goal in mind, the nature of the problem was relatively undefined. Such a broad challenge requires innovation leaders to work with a large canvas, with few constraints and great resources.

Large canvases are advantageous when ideationally competent leaders and their teams do not lack conceptual, financial, and time constraints in tackling the problem. The ability to think freely and apply generous resources toward a project enables the pursuit of a large canvas to be more successful. The team can hew to a specific direction, but team members are free to think more divergently than normal conditions would allow. Since ideationally competent leaders are pursuing a novel solution with a less defined path, working on a large canvas works best when there is the luxury of time. The more ambitious the desired innovation, the more time-consuming the ideation process will be.

While the results of a properly managed large canvas are impressive, too large of a canvas can have the effect of sprawling innovation teams. Bigger canvases can drive creativity, but they can also become overwhelming, even for the most skilled leader to manage. However, if utilized successfully, the long-term benefits of large-canvas innovation will allow an organization to thrive.

The iPhone was created using a large canvas. Steve Jobs knew that the portable phones on the market prior to 2007 were clunky and inconvenient to use, and he had a vision of something better. Bob Borcher, the first head of iPhone product marketing, recalled that when the product was in development, Jobs "wanted to create the first phone that people would fall in love with. That's what he told us. Now if you're an engineer, like I am by training, you're like 'what the heck does that mean?'"[85]

Jobs framed the challenge on a large canvas—to create a user-friendly device that could not only make phone calls but could also connect to the Internet and make use of a touch screen. With the gauntlet thrown down, Jobs gave the developers the creative space they needed to make the iPhone a reality. The first iPhone team would introduce, and continue to introduce, new features to change the notion of how a phone could be used. Through tackling a broad problem and allowing for abundant creativity, Steve Jobs succeeded in creating a device that is integral to daily life.

It may be important to constrain the canvas when innovations are too numerous or too ambitious. Steve Jobs was adept at framing and adapting the canvas. When he returned to Apple, he reduced its product line from 350 to ten: "Instead of creating 350 crappy products, or 200 mediocre products, or 100 good products Apple focused on creating 10 incredibly designed products."[86] Walter Isaacson recounts Jobs's process: "[Jobs] drew a two-by-two grid. 'Here's what we need,' he declared. Atop the two columns, he wrote 'Consumer' and 'Pro.' He labeled the two rows 'Desktop' and 'Portable.' Their job, he told his team members, was to focus on four great products, one for each quadrant. All other products should be canceled."[87]

Understanding the dangers of having sprawling innovation efforts, Jobs sought to narrow the canvas. This would allow his teams to dedicate their time and resources to perfecting a limited number of innovations instead of spreading out their efforts and ideas.

When leaders frame the canvas, they set boundaries for the divergent thinking required for the team's innovation. Defining a scope based on the various factors such as time, resources, and nature of the problem helps ideationally competent leaders pursue ideas that will be most relevant and useful within their organizational context.

## Lead for Ideation

To make sure that an idea thrives, it is not enough for leaders to simply frame the challenge. Rather, they must also lead for ideation effectively—that is, guide the ideation process. Ideationally competent leaders encourage the divergence of ideas under the chosen frame, resulting in a multitude of perspectives and potential innovations. Then they effectively cut through and prioritize, converging on the best ideas that can become concrete possibilities and move to prototype.

IDEO under the leadership of Tom Kelley is an organization capable of being open to and reading cues in its environment and translating them to concrete innovation. Framing the canvas is at the heart of how IDEO innovates. Its employees have helped design everything from a kid's toothbrush for Oral-B, to Apple's first mouse, to Kaiser Permanente's customer service process.[88]

A client approaches IDEO with a problem. Given the client's problem, IDEO decides how the problem shapes the canvas. A narrow canvas may be chosen such as "designing a toothbrush for kids" or a broader one like "helping improve patient experience at the hospital."

The company puts together a diverse team consisting of people from a range of backgrounds. In the case of Kaiser Permanente, "social scientists, designers, architects, and engineers"[89] were called in to work on the project. Team members come together to bring in the diverse perspectives that are necessary for successful divergence to occur. IDEO team members travel to the field to observe end-user issues and take the time to brainstorm solutions. To encourage the divergence process, all possible solutions are written on Post-it notes and displayed in a central location.

The final step is the convergence phase. Once multiple ideas are up on the wall, the IDEO team attempts to narrow them down to those that have the most potential. Often its members find interesting ways to combine various ideas to make an effective consolidated solution. Sometimes everyone votes for the top ideas, and they choose which one to concentrate their effort on. This is how the best ideas are chosen to prototype. At this point, the team incorporates consumer feedback into refining their prototype and testing it multiple times.

Through the process of ideation, using this notion of design thinking, the IDEO team ultimately arrives at an innovative solution that it delivers for its clients. If a key attribute of a thriving organization is to read cues in the environment and use the ideation process to transform those cues into products, services, and commodities, then IDEO is a superb example of a thriving organization, at least in terms of the dimension of discovery. Indeed, IDEO's approach to ideation and its institutionalization of divergent and convergent thinking is essential to breaking inertia.

## Divergence and Convergence: Get the Ideas

To break inertia, nothing is more important than getting the ideas out there and engaging in divergent thinking. Linus Pauling once remarked, "The way to get good ideas is to get lots of ideas and throw the bad ones away."[90] Pauling summarized divergent thinking. Robert Curedale, an expert in design thinking, amplifies Pauling's sentiments: "During the divergent phase of design the designer creates a number of choices. The goal of this approach is to analyze alternative approaches to test for the most stable solution. Divergent thinking is what we do when we do not know the answer."[91]

To diverge is to "get lots of ideas" and stick them on the canvas (or, like IDEO, write them on sticky notes and post them on a board). Here the innovation leader encourages people to move beyond the set standards and create more options. People are reminded to view things from different perspectives. They are inspired to use their imagination and tasked with inquiring and wandering into new territories. Innovation leaders encourage their team members to challenge the status quo and raise opposing ideas as a means of thinking about new possibilities.

To lead for divergence, ideationally competent leaders help their teams avoid biases and challenge assumptions by asking them the right questions. They make sure their team is conscious of hidden or unknown variables. Hidden biases sometimes constrain the creative process. Ideationally competent leaders raise awareness that frees the group. They are curious: they pry and interrogate. This is particularly difficult in organizations with myopic tendencies, in which case questions sometimes open a Pandora's box or are coded as being threatening. In these instances, the questions may deal with some of the taken-for-granted premises and assumptions or touch on one or more of the traps that may have resulted in inertia.

In organizations saddled with myopic tendencies, divergent ideas may create anxiety and resistance. In organizations beset with clunky tendencies, turf paranoia may create similar anxiety and resistance. That said, to break inertia, questioning is essential. As norms, standards, and old processes and ideas are revisited, new prospects and new avenues for innovation are opened. Leaders who create a culture of safety seed the ground for divergent thinking.

Tesla's leaders are ideationally competent and created a culture of safety. Breaking into new territory, and doing what's never been done before, means making mistakes. For them, "learning in an environment of uncertainty requires a willingness to admit mistakes and move quickly rather than digging in and doing nothing for fear of admitting failure. In fact, obsessively attempting to avoid failure can lead to the greater failure of missing the big opportunity."[92]

Through constructive questioning and discussion, ideationally competent leaders try to move discovery by safely engaging others around a series of challenges, encouraging them to explore, see different angles, visualize obstacles, and assess challenges. By creating a safe environment, protected from criticism and negative judgment, leaders give individuals a chance to have truly creative divergent input. Idea creation is encouraged, and robust delivery is ensured.

Ideationally competent leaders encourage experimentation in the organization. They don't negate ideas outright, but they build on the suggestions of others and encourage people to work beyond social familiarities. They know that their team needs to work beyond their comfort zone—and that staying close to the comfortable and familiar can lead to cognitive impairment. Familiarity breeds contempt, if not complacency. Ideationally competent leaders understand that to break inertia, diversity in background, experience, and perspective is the key to divergence. These leaders are not afraid of outliers, but welcome them.

Pragmatic leaders make use of divergent-thinking techniques to maximize off-the-wall ideas and push boundaries. Google is known for practicing "10x Thinking," which is "about trying to improve something by 10 times rather than by 10%."[93] By encouraging big thinking, team members can come up with radical solutions. The goal is to break down established processes and thought patterns to come up with many varied innovative ideas.

When the iPad was still in the germination stage, Steve Jobs had difficulty articulating what it would do: "Would it be just an iPhone with a bigger screen or would it have its own set of apps that set it apart?"[94] Jobs's bias was toward the former. He was not warm to the idea of the device becoming an "e-book reader, like the Kindle."[95] Months of discussion and debate followed, where he actively engaged in divergent thinking with the iPad team to flesh out the final concept.

Phil Schiller, head of global marketing "pushed Jobs to modify his view of what a 'consumption device' really meant." The reality was that the users needed the capacity to make changes to the "document, spreadsheet, and PowerPoint" they were accessing.[96] Additionally, Eddy Cue, the head of iTunes, was passionate about leveraging it as a platform for reading e-books: "When I got my first chance to touch the iPad, I became completely convinced that this was a huge opportunity for us to build the best e-reader that the market had ever seen."[97]

Ideationally competent leaders are also not afraid to be agnostic. That is, they don't just publicize their position and expect others to salute. They are careful to hear the views of all comers. Innovation leaders understand that traditions, values, and processes are important, but they are not afraid to challenge them. Innovation leaders allow the discomfort of holding contradictory thoughts.

While appreciating the power and synergy of divergent thinking and creating an environment where many ideas come to the surface, ideation leaders understand that a decision has to be made on which idea to move forward, which agenda to pursue, and what prototype to fund. Simply put, they have to decide where to place their bet. Therefore, they must lead for convergence.

Luc de Brabandere and Alan Iny frame the challenge of convergence: "Convergence requires you to evaluate your ideas, choose the most promising among them, and then zero in on which should be implemented, or in what order you think they should be pursued.[98] To select the ideas worthy of investment, out of the dozens or hundreds collected, ideationally competent leaders evaluate them using criteria of clarity, usability, workability, stability, long-term impact, profitability, integration, and scalability. They may define parameters, standards, and threshold levels of performance.

For example, the thinking may go something like this: the investment should be less than $1 million, the breakeven should be within three years, or speed should increase by 20 percent. Innovation leaders may look at what ideas have the potential to become the most disruptive or most successful in their respective markets. Some organizations ask employees to vote on the best ideas. Others have different teams submit their proposals to a panel of executives who evaluate the proposals and decide which ones to support. No matter how convergence is conducted, at the end of it, innovation leaders will have a handful of ideas that they are willing to back with the necessary resources.

Steve Jobs was a firm believer in the principle of convergence. He said, "I'm actually as proud of the things we haven't done as the things I have done. Innovation is saying 'no' to 1,000 things."[99] Jobs exhibited this when focusing ideas during one of the first Top 100 retreats. On the last day, he asked the group: "'What are the 10 things we should be doing next?' People would fight to get their suggestions on the list. Jobs would write them down—and then cross off the ones he decreed dumb. After much jockeying, the group would come up with a list of 10. Then Jobs would slash the bottom seven and announce, 'We can only do three.'"[100]

Clearly, Jobs had mastered the art of convergence. By deciding on a few great ideas, he could dedicate resources to their development, creating innovative and disruptive products that led to Apple's success.

## Maintain Hot Group Culture

While leaders can deal with the structural problems that inhibit information flow and enhance idea formation through the ideation process of divergent and convergent thinking, ideationally competent leaders know that nothing is more important in breaking inertia than creating the culture of collective excitement. Nothing captures the essence of the culture of innovation better than a hot group, a naturally forming collective of task-obsessed and highly innovative individuals that often deliver astonishing results. Hot groups demonstrate the power of the collective to innovate and perform. A hot group culture can be essential in stimulating innovation while maintaining a culture of synergy, passion, and innovation motivation. Through the collective social-psychological power of hot groups, innovation can move forward and inertia can be broken.

"Hot group" is a term that developed in the 1990s to describe teams who not only worked tremendously well together, but also achieved great things in a relatively compressed time frame due to task-focused passion. A classic example of a hot group is the NASA control room in Houston when the Apollo 13 crew faced a near calamity. When an explosion in the spacecraft damaged two oxygen tanks, venting oxygen into outer space, the mission to the moon became an emergency rescue operation. The control room sprang alive and became a miraculous, organic, problem-solving unit—essentially operating as an incredibly efficient hot group. All ideas focused on reaching a solution to the problem. Role differentiation vanished, task specificity became diffuse, and any notion of a plan went by the wayside. Flight director Gene Krantz gave the parameters of the assignment ahead of them: "Let's work on the problem, people. Let's not make things worse by guessing."[101] Working together, the team was able to improvise ingenious solutions. Jack Lousma, the capsule communicator, recalls, "We just responded as we had to. . . . It was dynamic, people working real hard to find out what the problems were. It was a bunch of people who were trying to solve these problems as they came up."[102]

The group brought together the core elements of a hot group: the sense of the importance of their mission, passion, teamwork, hard work, and a cast of very skilled individuals. While many in the group were initially assigned to specific tasks, the rules of the game quickly changed. The mission became complex, urgent, and intensely captivating, pulling together resources and bright minds to work around the multitude of limitations. With incredible time pressure and an impossibly complicated task, the group worked feverishly to deliver results. In retrospect, "the most remarkable achievement of mission control was quickly developing procedures for powering up the CM [control module] after its long, cold sleep. Flight controllers wrote the documents for this innovation in three days, instead of the usual three months."[103]

Jean Lipman-Blumen and Harold Leavitt claim that "any group can be a hot group"—so long as it has the "distinctive state of mind," which they define as "task-obsessed and full of passion." This mind-set is "coupled with a distinctive way of behaving, a style that is intense, sharply focused, and full-bore."[104]

Most often, hot groups form around an idea. An individual may come up with an idea that gathers excitement, with others who may not be officially tasked to work together, forming a group that gains "heat"[105] around that idea. Hence comes the natural formation of a hot group, a group that is incredibly passionate, filled with purpose, and intrinsically motivated to achieve results.

Tom Kelley of IDEO defines hot groups as "great teams" who are "totally dedicated to achieving the end result." They are "irreverent and non-hierarchical ... [and] well rounded and respective of [group members'] diversity." In addition, Kelley says, the ideal hot group works "in an open eclectic space optimal for flexibility, group work and brainstorming."[106]

Hot groups are passionate, dedicated to solving a problem or attaining a specific outcome. Hot groups value autonomy and freedom of information flow, as well as diverse skill sets and perspectives. The focus of hot group members enables them to conquer deadlines that most would find difficult at best. Hot group leaders sustain the interest of the group and instill the sense that their work is important to reinforce their commitment to the pursuit of the problem. Hot groups often lack hierarchy, and as such, they are not burdened by unnecessary bureaucracy.

Effective hot groups are noteworthy for their diversity. Their members tend to come from many areas of an organization—a combination of generalists, specialists, and polymaths is best for creating a high-quality innovative culture. These various skill sets enhance their ability to collectively think outside the box. Hot group members tend to be comfortable with going outside their organization to gather data, opinions, and ideas. As Kelley notes, hot groups work better in an open and elastic space, allowing their members to modify it to their liking, as a prologue to innovation.

Autonomy and the ability to pursue interesting projects are a huge factor in the formation of hot groups. Hot groups assume that employees will be more dedicated and have more freedom to be creative when they have intrinsic motivation for the project they are pursuing rather than when they simply complete tasks to meet forced business goals. Some organizations embed the hot group philosophy in their structure and culture.

Employees at the gaming company Valve have the freedom to work on any project that piques their interest. One staffer notes, "People ask you questions about what you are working on. And the response is not to get defensive but to have that conversation and make sure that we're all invested in each other."[107] Employees form teams based on either a specific game or a specific feature that needs to be implemented for a game. Once it is completed, teams are free to re-form around new projects, as defined by the necessities of the problem at hand. Even Valve employees' desks are fully mobile. They have wheels that allow them to relocate and form a team with someone on another floor simply by moving their entire workstation.[108] As interest forms around a specific project, it will attract people and form an enthusiastic, problem-solving team, capable of pushing an innovation to execution effectively. Valve's projects are populated with people who either are passionate about what is being worked on or feel that they can contribute to it. Those who see themselves as a better fit elsewhere will not feel forced to participate in something they have no interest in. At Valve, hot groups are malleable and very much project based.

The scientists and engineers at Bell Labs are well known for functioning in hot groups. Individual team members and project leads possessed a good deal of skill diversity and creativity: "Bell Labs' senior managers were not managers in the traditional sense: They were outstanding engineers and scientists who demanded discipline and responsibility on the one hand, while encouraging creativity and communication on the other."[109]

In terms of leveraging the power of the collective, the senior managers encouraged every scientist and researcher to air their ideas, no matter how far out or inconsequential. They understood that the next great discovery could spring from any direction. In fact, the senior managers encouraged their team members to increase their idea generation: "At Bell Labs, they [team members] were highly valued and encouraged to pursue whatever they believed to be the most interesting avenues of scientific inquiry."[110]

Leaders at Bell Labs worked toward eliminating or reducing the barriers of innovation. They brought together creative individuals in groups and leveraged the talents of the collective team. Their approach to innovation led to an incredible period of sustained innovation, ranging from the development of "communications satellites; the theory and development of digital communications; and the first cellular telephone systems."[111]

It may be incredibly difficult to purposefully create a genuine hot group, as individuals within hot groups generally have a very high level of intrinsic motivation and passion for their idea. Indeed, hot groups emerge naturally in an environment where there is a fluidity of ideas. If there is one prerequisite for the emergence of a hot group, it is the creation a culture where ideas are free-floating and available to everyone, and linkages between creative people are unhampered. Today, there are numerous platforms and processes that organizations can use to facilitate the formation of a hot group culture.

For example, Ericsson's IdeaBoxes online platform is an effective way to not only promote idea sharing but also generate the excitement of following and watching a friend or colleague's idea grow. IdeaBoxes can be described as a social networking site for innovation and idea sharing, or a supercharged suggestion box. Not only can employees create a box, but they can comment on other boxes, or they can do a keyword search to see if anyone is already working on a given problem.[112] As Magnus Karlsson, a key innovator for IdeaBoxes, notes, "We wanted to let ideas travel freely throughout the different silos of the organization."[113] A platform such as IdeaBoxes can aid and accelerate the formation of hot groups as ideas are more free to spread and others are encouraged to help develop and build ideas together, creating an air of excitement and enthusiasm around powerful ideas.

Hackathons allow for the situation, space, and time for hot groups to be created: "A hackathon is an event which has become synonymous with software and hardware development teams collaborating and coming together to create something new, or to solve a particular problem given to them, typically the event lasting anything between a day and a week."[114]

Hackathon sponsors create an environment of collaboration, safety, and purpose to support focused passion. Hackathons are often built around a specific theme or direction. While attendees may not be drawn initially to a specific idea, they are passionate about the topic at large. Groups then form around ideas and projects based on the group member's individual skills and interests. These groups also tend to come in with high synergy. Hackathons can allow employees and individuals to function as hot groups. Task-focused ideation and rapid innovation is a result of the passion and creative energy at a hackathon, as well as the safety to promote divergent ideas.

Toy manufacturer Hasbro sponsored its first hackathon in 2013. Organizer Sadeen Ali reported that in two days, "150 developers came and developed 45 products—equivalent to billions of dollars in traditional R&D."[115] Large organizations such as Cognizant, Facebook, Google, Microsoft, and Netflix hold hackathons for innovation.[116] A side benefit of a corporate hackathon open to nonemployees is that there is a chance for leaders to spot and try out new talent.[117]

Hackathons are not only important for product development, but they "can be adapted to greatly accelerate the process of digital transformation. They are less about designing new products and more about 'hacking' away at old processes and ways of working. By giving management and others the ability to kick the tires of collaborative design practices, 24-hour hackathons can show that big organizations are capable of delivering breakthrough innovation at start-up speed."[118]

Hackathons are a way to "embrace the principle of 'fail fast, succeed faster' and accept failure as part of the development process."[119] To draw on the observation of Dave Fontenot: "To sum it up, at a hackathon, people come together and use technology to transform ideas into reality."[120]

Twitter is the offspring of a hackathon and a hot group. The future founders of Twitter were working at the start-up Odeo and tasked with building a platform for podcasts. With Apple's launch of iTunes, combined with the fading popularity of podcasts and radio, the employees at Odeo began to feel discouraged.[121] Enthusiasm waned as it seemed like the company was headed into trouble. The CEO started hosting official hackathons with the intent of generating ideas for new directions to pursue, and Twitter was one such idea.

Jack Dorsey had the idea of a social network revolving around status updates. Pitching his idea to coworkers and influencers in the organization, he convinced Odeo cofounder Noah Glass to see the potential. The two became incredibly passionate about the project: "There were two people who were really excited [about Twitter], Jack and Noah Glass. Noah was fanatically excited about Twitter. Fanatically!"[122] They formed a small team to work on the new project, dubbed Twttr.

The team spent most of their energy on the project. What started as an idea for a side project became a force to be reckoned with as talented and driven team members pushed it to success. Today, Twitter is ubiquitous in the social media arena, and Odeo has all but vanished from the Internet space.

▲  ▲  ▲

Having picked up the contextual cues in the environment and explored the signals and trends, obstacles and challenges, ideationally competent leaders support the internal process of innovation. They have the ideational competence to create the sense of sharing, the sense of risk-taking, the sense of direction that transforms initial trend insights into concrete innovations and prototypes. In doing so, they must foster information flow, frame the challenges appropriately, lead the ideation process, and sustain a hot group culture. These are the pragmatic leadership skills of robust discovery, allowing the organization to overcome inertia caused by myopic or clunky tendencies. Without these skills, hunches, insights, and trends will be lost in the organizational void.

# 3

# LEADING FOR FOCUSED DELIVERY

## CAMPAIGN FOR SUPPORT

The initial discovery phase may go a long way in breaking inertia. However, this is only the beginning. The inception of an idea—its discovery—is not sufficient on its own to break organizational inertia. Ideas may surface, emerge as a complete prototype, and meet all criteria of success, but if leaders don't campaign for their good ideas and move them through the organizational maze, they'll drop the ball. Pragmatic leaders know that good ideas are not enough. To overcome inertia their challenge is to move agendas and get ideas through the eye of the needle.[1]

In most organizations, the process of discovery rarely results in active resistance. Before the idea is tangible, it can't be a perceived threat to the status quo. However, the moment that a specific idea shows its concrete potential, the forces of resistance jump into action. Resistance is "an act of refraining from adoption"[2] of any change proposal that challenges the status quo interests of groups, units, and individuals in the organization. No matter how good the idea or how worthy the agenda, one person or one group's priorities may not be aligned with the priorities of another person or group. The challenge

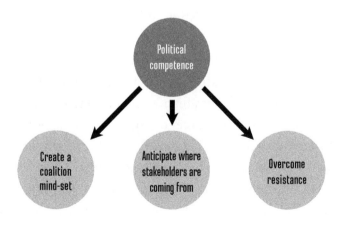

for campaigners is to have the political competence to campaign to win support and coalesce.

The sources of resistance are innumerable. No matter how good an idea is or how rigorously it's been tested, there is no guarantee it will get to the next level. In clunky organizations issues of turf, transaction costs, and fear of losing power can lead to resistance. When the myopic tendency is in play, the fear of losing face or the security that comes from habit will cause many leaders to retreat into accepted business models and the old ways of doing things to preserve some semblance of safety. In the context of political inertia that arises from clunky and myopic tendencies, leaders need to be campaigners and masters of political competence. Leaders who are campaigners create a coalition mind-set, anticipate the power and agendas of stakeholders, and overcome the hesitation of those whose support they need.

## Create a Coalition Mind-Set

A key to breaking political resistance and inertia is to establish a coalition mind-set. For an organization to thrive, to simply talk about collaboration and cooperation may not be enough. To have the support to drive ideas through the organizational maze, leaders need to achieve a cohesive coalescing collaboration. What does it mean to coalesce?

In most organizational settings, individuals tend to have continuous cooperative relationships with each other. This is a type of amorphous collaboration. Coalescing is much more purposeful. A coalition in this context is a conscious alliance mobilized to pursue a specific goal or aim. Individual employees or organizational subunits get together to work toward a specific goal. Examples of coalitions may be individuals who are dedicated to pursing a new market strategy in the Far East or the group wishing to implement a new learning platform for the business school. To move a specific agenda or project, focused mindful collaboration in the form of a coalition must take place.

With intent and common purpose, a coalition focuses on a defined goal. The leadership challenge for pragmatic leaders trying to break inertia is to establish a coalition mind-set to gain support in the pursuit of a new idea, innovation, change, or agenda. This means breaking down the embedded interests of individual subunits and giving them, at least in the short term, a common point for collaboration. The creation of a common purpose around a defined goal is accomplished through the pragmatic leadership capacity of individual campaigners. Only through political competence can campaigners establish a coalition mind-set that can ensure robust delivery and implementation. Politically competent leaders break down the embedded interests of individuals and units and give them a common point of collaboration.

David Krackhardt's research indicates that when a controversial innovation is introduced, the campaigner will find more success focusing on a peripheral subunit or cluster.[3] The secluded nature of the subunit will protect the innovation from backlash and will allow early adopters to try out the innovation before it is introduced to a larger (and perhaps hostile) audience.[4]

As the above exemplifies, when moving agendas, organizational leaders need to be pragmatically political. They appreciate that by introducing a new idea to too many stakeholders and resistant subunits at once, the innovation is highly likely to be shut down right away. However, a leader who is a campaigner, as Krackhardt's analysis implies, would seed the innovation to a peripheral group or a coalition, allowing the innovation to make its way throughout the network at its own pace and create its own momentum. The proposal for the innovation needs to be tailored to address the specific needs and concerns of each new stakeholder, instead of facing the impossible challenge of satisfying many stakeholders at once.

To break inertia, organizations need leaders who can form coalitions and use the coalitions to push agendas, ideas, and innovations through the organizational maze. To do this, they must identify key stakeholders and influencers. Without the political competence to campaign, even the best ideas will go nowhere. Microsoft under Steve Ballmer struggled to implement innovative ideas. Faced with stubborn and change-resistant leadership, employees found it difficult to get the initial buy-in necessary to push innovation forward.

During the 2000s, Microsoft was the home of two fiefdoms—Windows and Office. As the primary sources of revenue, resources poured into both units, and power followed. The unwritten rule was that new products had to be supported by the leaders of either division. The official explanation was that "compatibility" was the watchword. After all, compatibility guaranteed that the company remained profitable, at least in the short run.

The leaders of the Windows and Office divisions wielded enormous power and could kill projects that they deemed unworthy and unimportant. The inertia bias reigned, especially if there were challenges to the status quo: "When younger employees tried to point out emerging trends among their friends, supervisors sometimes just waved them away."[5] Protecting their resources and preserving their dominance in the organization superseded the pursuit of innovation. Anyone trying to move an agenda at Microsoft needed to create a coalition to attract support from leaders in the organization, but with entrenched, competing interests, moving an agenda became nearly impossible in the rigid, hierarchical framework of Microsoft. Consequently, true innovation was a rarity.

The failure to build a coalition contributed to the company's inability to update MSN Messenger with the features necessary to compete effectively with AIM (AOL Instant Messenger).[6] Before the social media revolution got into full swing, a young Microsoft developer noticed that his friends "signed up for AIM exclusively and left it running most of the time," because they wanted "to use the program's status message, which allowed them to type a short note telling their online buddies what they were doing, even if they weren't at the computer." The developer's revelation was that the "main purpose of AIM wasn't to chat, but to give you the chance to log in at any time and check out what your friends were doing."[7]

By connecting the dots, the young developer predicted that virtually none of his cohort would switch to MSN Messenger because it lacked this feature. When he presented his concerns to his supervisor, his ambition to update the program was quickly dismissed: "Why would young people care about putting up a few words? Anyone who wanted to tell friends what they were doing could write it on their profile page."[8] The manager didn't understand the essence of instant messaging, and the young developer, without having the political skills to push ideas forward, was forced to admit defeat. The consequence was that Microsoft missed the social media boat, when it could have been an agile competitor against Facebook and Google in this arena.[9]

As in the case of Microsoft, coalitions are necessary for the intrapreneur who has an idea that pushes the envelope and stretches the organization beyond its current boundaries. In fact, coalitions are necessary for moving change in organizations of all types, but they are essential in organizations that are in the habit of building incrementally on already established ideas. Because there isn't a big push to "get it done," inertia has the tendency to set in. The coalition mindset is necessary to break inertia.

Take the case of Sony and its attempts to change its design process during the development of the PlayStation 4. For years, Sony dominated the gaming industry. When its predecessor, the PlayStation 3, was released, "Sony controlled about 70 percent of the console market."[10] However, its market dominance led to the emergence of silos emblematic of entrenched clunky tendencies. When Sony was at its zenith, its hardware and software divisions competed for resources and rarely coordinated their activities. It was often the case that the company's hardware divisions took precedence over software, impeding true collaboration and integration.

This is exactly what plagued the development of the PlayStation 3. Launched in 2006, the console boasted the most powerful hardware on the market. However, its complex, obscure architecture made it difficult to create games for the system. Because the software developers were not invited to offer feedback on the development of the system, "the PS3 launched with only 12 game titles, and most didn't take full advantage of its Cell microprocessor." Predictably, the PlayStation 3 failed to gain traction, and the unit was overshadowed by Microsoft's "Xbox 360 [which] outsold the PS3 in the U.S. for 32 consecutive months."[11]

To their credit, Sony's leaders were aware of the shortcomings caused by the company's clunky tendency. During the development of the PlayStation 4, Sony's leaders deliberately fostered the coalition mind-set to ensure that history would not repeat itself. One key decision was to appoint Mark Cerney, an experienced game designer, to oversee the development of the console's hardware. Cerney's role was to "right the wrongs of the PS3." His first order of business was to reach out to game design studios, within and external to Sony, to build a coalition. Cerney recalls, "I did something that would have been unthinkable in 2004: I went to about 30 game teams about what they would like to see in the next-generation hardware."[12]

Cerney established a coalition mind-set by promising game developers that their input would be directed to and used by the leaders of Sony's hardware divisions. Cerney's goal was simple: "The thought was that we would start with a more open process, a more collaborative look at what worked and what didn't."[13] By knocking down the clunky wall that created turf battles between hardware and software, he created a coalition and broke inertia. Developers not only find it less challenging to develop games for the PlayStation 4, but the console is also affordable: "Its retail price is just under $400—$100 less than the new Xbox One—and thanks to its relatively simple design, the console is launching alongside a slate of 22 new game titles."[14] Sony's PlayStation continues to outsell its Microsoft competitor. Cerney's coalition has paid off.

The turnaround of AIG provides another example of the importance of forming a coalition. AIG was left gasping for breath in the wake of the 2007 financial crisis when the government stepped in with a bailout of $182 billion. Leadership was in disarray and employee morale was at an all-time low. Bob Benmosche, the fourth CEO in less than a year, came on the scene in 2009. His agenda was to turn around AIG. He needed to position AIG for growth and to pay back its loans. He built a coalition with the board and AIG's employees to unite the company.

Benmosche's first challenge was to coalesce the board under his vision. The board was split between those who wanted to IPO a subsidiary and those, along with Benmosche, who wanted to sell the subsidiary. The opposition, led by the chairman Harvey Golub, did all they could to deny any possibility of selling the subsidiary. Benmosche realized he could not convert Golub and that Golub would be a resisting factor. Benmosche recalls, "I said you see things one way, I see things another way. So I think we need to reconcile where we are and whether we can move forward. It was very clear he and I didn't see eye to eye."[15] Benmosche gave the board an ultimatum: choose him or Golub. Golub resigned. From then on the board was behind Benmosche's initiatives, including the sale of the subsidiary.

Benmosche's second coalition was with AIG employees. He need-ed them to believe the organization had a future and would fulfill its commitments to them. Benmosche's predecessor, Edward Liddy, failed to protect his employees at the height of the crisis. Jake De-Santis, an executive vice president of AIG's financial products unit, wrote in a public resignation letter, "I am disappointed and frustrated over your lack of support for us. I and many others in the unit feel betrayed that you failed to stand up for us in the face of untrue and unfair accusations from certain members of Congress last Wednesday and from the press over our retention payments."[16] Benmosche took decisive action to retain and motivate his employees. He told the financial products employees, "I want you to understand what happened will not happen again."[17] He also held town-hall meetings with employees to reassure them that they would be paid for their work, that AIG's debt would be paid off, and that they had a future at AIG. Many employees found Bob Benmosche to be a strong leader and remained with the company.

Eventually AIG paid off its debt in full and restored its stock market value. Benmosche's efforts were hailed as "one of the greatest financial turnarounds in American corporate history."[18] By creating a coalition mind-set and getting the support he needed from the board and employees, Benmosche was able to execute his plan and vision for AIG.

As these examples illustrate, competing interests are part and parcel of any complex organization. Some units are more entrenched and have more prestige and power than others. If the initiative proposes to take resources from the A team, politically competent leaders know that they have their work cut out for them. Once they have developed their agenda or innovation, politically competent leaders need to figure out how to get others to join their effort and have them form a supportive coalition.

Pragmatic leaders who have political competence understand that the creation of a coalition to move any major idea is essential. They understand that to create a coalition, they need to examine the organizational arena to anticipate where stakeholders are coming from and negotiate to form a coalition.

## Anticipate Where Stakeholders Are Coming From

In an organization with clunky tendencies, there are many independent factions—units, departments, and individuals—that wield autonomous power to pursue and protect their priorities. In some instances, the power network may not be evident, but it lurks beneath the surface. In the context of a clunky organization with its diverse array of interests or a myopic organization with its entrenchment, it is essential to discern who is likely join the campaign and who may have some hesitation. To break inertia created by the anarchy of the clunky tendency or the blinder traps of the myopic tendency, pragmatic leaders develop a methodical understanding of where others are coming from. Both situations demand that politically competent leaders master the skills of anticipation.

Anticipation implies the capacity to identify the key stakeholders—internal and external to their organization—who have an interest in the success of their agenda and who likely have a position or strong opinion about their approach. It is the capacity to understand where other key stakeholders and key units are coming from. To overcome inertia and establish a coalition mind-set, politically competent leaders focus not simply on their power and their agendas, but also the power and agendas of other stakeholders.

### Identify the Power Stakeholders

In a complex organizational setting, the first factor that politically competent leaders anticipate is the power held by potential allies and resisters. They distinguish between those who have authority, the formal capacity to give the thumbs up or down for a specific agenda, and those who have influence, the informal capacity to help move an idea. In contemporary organizations, with authority more centralized and restricted, and influence more diffuse, anticipating the type of power that potential allies and resisters have is essential.[19]

Top dogs—those who have the final say and the capacity to say yea or nay to any suggestion—headline the list. Top dogs have the title, the authority, and the paycheck that let others know that they have power. They can green-light the agenda or they can stop it cold. Ultimately, top dogs have the capacity to dictate the direction of the organization. For smaller initiatives, the support of the top dog isn't crucial, but if a proposed project is ambitious, the support—even passive support—of the top dog is essential. Sometimes the interests of tops dogs, especially those who have been in power for an extended period, are entrenched. That said, other top dogs may feel that because of their direct accountability they need to ensure that the organization is not trapped by inertia but is, indeed, thriving. Understanding the power and intentions of the top dog is critical.

Next in line are the gatekeepers. The power of gatekeepers is diffuse and fragmented. They have influence over a specific arena, but more important, they are the link between the top dog(s) and the rest of the organization. Though gatekeepers may report to a top dog, they may have independent control over one or two areas in the organization. The power of gatekeepers stems from their proximity to resources and authority figures. Gatekeepers can be found in groups, like senior management or the finance committee, but in smaller organizations, there may be just one gatekeeper. When approaching a gatekeeper, politically competent leaders need to be prepared to fully brief them on their project proposal. It is important to win the support of gatekeepers. With influential gatekeepers on board, others in the organization will be more likely to join the effort.

Gurus form the third category of influencers. While not always in traditional positions of authority, these individuals can be critical in the push for innovative change. Gurus can be powerful outsiders with formal or informal authority within the organization or they can be powerful insiders with great technological or other expertise that is essential to the organization. A guru could be a semiretired vice president or an external consultant who is close to senior management but has a strong view or opinion. A guru can be a valued employee with specialized expertise. In some cases, gurus could be the board of directors or other individuals who have some pull with the decision makers. While gurus are often on the fringes of organizational life, they are uniquely placed because they have a relationship with the senior people and may not be afraid to register their pleasure—or displeasure—with a specific agenda. It is frequently the case that gurus have been around since the organization's early days. While their technical expertise may have faded, they have the power of institutional knowledge on their side and their support may be essential to getting anything done.

Players are the everyday organizational members whose specific activities will be directly touched by any change agenda. While players do not have formal authority, they can influence how an agenda is implemented. Players, with their deep technical expertise, have the potential to be detractors or supporters. Politically competent leaders are careful to give players the attention they deserve. A player who is discounted or ignored could do damage to any change agenda. In any organization, players outnumber top dogs, gatekeepers, and gurus.

Breaking inertia is about the process of mobilizing and getting traction with those in positions of power, getting them to join the coalition, and gathering more and more support over time. In a myopic organization, power may be embedded with the top dogs and there may be a false, almost paranoid sense, that everything must be run by the top dog before proceeding, which can stifle innovation. In a clunky organization, when authority emerges from many quarters, it is sometimes difficult to bring the right people on board at the right time, and it's often difficult to know who the top dog in charge is.

Politically competent leaders are classic agenda movers. They take their time to do their homework. They classify the stakeholders, and they understand whose support they need to successfully implement their agenda. They know that campaigning is essential to overcoming resistance and breaking inertia, and that campaigning begins with understanding the power players.

Lee Iacocca was a campaigner who did just that. As the new general manager at the Ford Motor Company in the early 1960s, Iacocca was a gatekeeper. He knew he was in the perfect position to investigate the feasibility of the Mustang concept. As such, he campaigned accordingly. He recognized that he needed to map the political terrain to get a better understanding of the type of support he needed.

Iacocca first pulled together a team of influential Ford engineers to work on the concept for the new car. Every member of the team was a guru in his own right, a superstar with a unique and exciting perspective. By tapping gurus such as Harold Sperlich and getting them on his side, Iacocca harnessed their genius and creativity.

In addition to mapping and recruiting gurus, Iacocca turned his attention to Ford's players, the engineers and designers. Iacocca opened up the design process: "Believing that competition spurred creativity, Iacocca organized an in-house contest. Designers from the Ford division, the Lincoln-Mercury division, and Ford's Advance Projects department were pitted against each other."[20] Iacocca's plan worked spectacularly, as the designers bought into the Mustang and competed to create the best car: "The stylists got caught up in the excitement and, in just three weeks, had six different proposals."[21] The ultimate Mustang design came from these efforts.

Finally, Iacocca knew that he needed one more person on his side,

CEO Henry Ford II, the top dog who could potentially sink his project. He had worked on the project for months before formally approaching Ford: "With the basic design and name set, there was still one person to convince—the one person who could cancel the whole project. Henry Ford II gave his blessing in September 1962 with just three caveats: 1.) It had to be built for $45 million rather than the $75 million Iacocca asked, 2.) It needed an inch more legroom in the backseat and 3.) It had to sell."[22]

And sell it did. Iacocca was a consummate campaigner who mapped the political terrain. Instead of attempting to gain support of everyone at once, he gradually gained the support of key stakeholders and influencers from all over the organization. He was able to get gurus on his side to help guide the initial concept. He then moved on to harnessing the power of players to develop a concrete proposal. When the pieces were place, he made a carefully articulated appeal to the top dog who held decisive power over the project. The successful launch of the Mustang was a testament to Iacocca's political competence.

## Determine Core Agenda Styles

Knowing simply who has influence and authority is not enough to break inertia. Politically competent leaders mobilize the support of others by anticipating their specific agendas. In thinking about the agendas of others, they deal with the core intent of a group or individual. They analyze the agendas of potential allies and resisters by considering not only their short-term intentions but also by thinking about how they prefer to make adjustments and how accepting they are to change.[23]

Organizations, groups, and individuals have varying degrees of comfort with change. At one end of the continuum there are tinkerers, who prefer conservative, incremental change, and at the other end are the overhaulers, who prefer more drastic change. The tension between these different approaches is likely to be manifested as resistance as a change agenda is being introduced and moved. Resistance can be very subtle. It is unlikely that there will be a chorus of "no way" and "forget about it" when an idea is introduced. What happens is that obstacles are created and thrown in the path of change that will cast doubt on the potential success of the initiative.

In an organizational context, the biases of tinkerers and overhaulers inform their resistance to change. For instance, the slow-moving tinkerer will accuse the overhauler of moving too fast and not taking the time to thoroughly analyze the current situation. Tinkerers are prone to panic when there isn't an iceberg in sight. Tinkerers tend to be risk averse, with a preference for making changes in specific and controlled ways. They target opportunities to achieve operational efficiencies and incremental improvements. That is, they are likely to use a small canvas when tackling a problem.

Overhaulers insist that tinkerers move too slowly, rearrange deck chairs on the Titanic, or ignore the realities of the market. Overhaulers tend to be concerned with making fundamental changes rather than incremental improvements. They insist on new directions and trajectories, breaking down old processes. They are likely to look for longer-term benefits and implement a larger canvas when tackling a problem.

This conflict over the preferred agenda can be a source of inertia. Politically competent leaders are aware of these tendencies and take them into account when moving from group to group trying to mobilize support for the innovation or change agenda.

There is some variation in the scope of tinkering and overhauling that individuals and groups are comfortable with. Tinkerers may be *traditionalists*, or they may be change-accepting *adjusters*. Overhaulers may be *revolutionaries* or they may be *developers*.

The stereotypical tinkerer may have a traditionalist style. A stakeholder with a traditionalist agenda may attribute the sorry current state of their organization to a "breakdown of tradition." Therefore, they agree with any change effort that gets the organization back on track and returns it to the old ways. Additionally, traditionalists prefer taking small actions backed by detailed plans. Their cautiousness and reflective nature may be temporarily reassuring in that they tend to support the status quo. However, traditionalists may overlook crucial differences between past and present circumstances. Stakeholders who consistently hew to a traditionalist mind-set may blind their organization from spotting and adapting to external threats and pursing lucrative opportunities. While a tinkering traditionalist agenda style may seem to be a hindrance to progress, it can be useful in controlling impulsive action and limiting risk.

Walter B. Hewlett, cofounder and former board member of Hewlett-Packard, was a true traditionalist.[24] When HP made the decision to merge with Compaq, Hewlett stood in lone opposition. He felt the merger would cause HP to sprawl into the low-profit PC market and damage HP's printer business, its crown jewel.

Hewlett insisted that he was not opposed to change per se, but rather disagreed with the merger strategy, which reflected a company-wide shift from one of focus to one of scale. Hewlett stated that "the fundamental mistake in the thinking behind the merger was the perceived need to do something with scale, instead of succeeding the way HP has in the past, with focus and innovation."[25]

Hewlett's opponents argued that the current turbulent environment required HP to become a "full service supplier of hardware, software, and services to large corporate customers,"[26] along the lines of IBM. This could be achieved only through the merger, which would allow HP to consolidate PC operations with Compaq; the new enterprise would dominate the PC market. From this perspective, Hewlett's traditionalist rhetoric was interpreted as being constraining and insensitive to the reality of the current business environment.

Hewlett was strongly criticized for being too resistant to change. Supporters, including stock analysts, investors, and strategists, thought Hewlett's perspective was right on the mark and exactly what HP needed during a volatile time.

On the other end of the spectrum, there are revolutionaries— those who have no problem tearing the envelope. The revolutionary agenda is based on the belief that radical change is an organizational necessity. Revolutionaries emphasize overhauling and the ability to adapt to change, even before it's apparent. Revolutionaries believe that elements of the current organization are fundamentally flawed. Although proponents of great change, they often can't be bothered with detailed planning. They prefer to plunge into the application of their agendas, making every effort to retain the flexibility necessary to improvise and react as the situation changes. Revolutionaries prefer agendas that push their organizations toward their absolute change limits. The revolutionary endgame looks nothing like what was in place originally.

Steve Jobs is hailed as a great revolutionary. He had a penchant for improvisation and grand, sweeping changes. He would shake things up, redirecting workflows and processes to fit his current agenda. That said, early on, he was much more stubborn when it came to under-standing the intricacies of organizational politics. Revolutionaries still need the support of others to push their broad agendas.

Jobs's initial exit from Apple was the direct result of his lack of political competence—specifically, his inability to empathize with and adapt to the agendas of his key stakeholders. During his initial stint at Apple, Jobs was the consummate explorer and innovator. His extraordinary efforts resulted in the Macintosh. While the comput-er drew accolades for its innovation, sales lagged: "The Mac debuted in 1984 to rave reviews but disappointing sales, putting a financial strain on the company—and fraying Jobs' relationship with [John] Sculley."[27] The initial release of the Macintosh was a fiasco. The next question was how to fix it.

Jobs had great faith not only in his capabilities, but also in the value of his creation. Jobs, the revolutionary, thought that the Macintosh was a solid product, a work of art that far outclassed its rivals. Instead of blaming the failed launch on the product itself, Jobs blamed its high price tag and its meager advertising budget. He advocated for a price cut and a redoubled marketing effort.[28] By making a radical shift in pricing and marketing, Jobs thought the Mac could be salvaged.

When it came to the Mac, Apple's then-CEO John Sculley and the company's board of directors were traditionalists. For them, the math was simple. Low initial sales equaled failure. Their preferred approach was to reinvest in the Apple II and dump the Mac. Sculley and the board understood the immense challenges associated with attempting to turn around a failing product. Unlike Jobs, they were unwilling to risk further failure and financial decline.

It was evident to Jobs that Sculley and the board resisted his proposal for a price drop and a change in advertising strategy. Jobs also correctly identified their traditionalist agendas and noted the narrow nature of their alternative proposal. However, in the face of clear opposition, Jobs made no attempt to modify his agenda and come up with a more moderate approach that would better satisfy the conservative agendas of Apple's primary stakeholders. Instead, he chose to stand his ground, resolutely retaining his staunch revolutionary agenda and resisting their efforts. In the ensuing power struggle between Sculley and Jobs, the board formed a coalition with Sculley, and Jobs was pushed out as head of the Mac division.[29] Jobs and Sculley could not align their divergent agendas, which may have been a factor that contributed to Apple's subsequent inertia.

While revolutionaries and traditionalists bookend the agenda continuum, there are other agendas that share the traits of each. Some stakeholders are admittedly conservative yet open to change—just nothing too big and too dramatic. Like their traditionalist cousins, those with an adjuster agenda prefer to tinker and tweak and fine-tune, but they are resistant to rigid planning. They understand the necessity for change when the need arises and trust ability to adapt. Adjusters carefully time their changes, rather than risk overreacting to the signals they pick up. Adjusters attempt to isolate the factors that demand pressing action, moving only when necessary.

After Jobs's death, Tim Cook took the reins of Apple. Cook is not the revolutionary his predecessor was, yet Apple continues to flourish. Cook is an adjuster, with a preference for making relatively small, yet fundamentally sound tweaks,[30] such as his decision to change the iPhone incrementally to be larger and slimmer, while competitors such as Samsung opted for more drastic changes that included the release of even larger smartphones with brighter OLED screens that lacked bezels.

Cook understands the necessity of improvising to make some broader change to keep Apple relevant. The Apple Watch, not necessarily a radical product or produced with a long lead time, was a reaction to the burgeoning wearable technology trend.[31] Cook is comfortable making improvised, yet tinkering changes to Apple's product line. Uncharacteristically for Apple, Cook took a chance in acquiring audio company Beats Electronics for $3 billion.[32] Cook can assess areas for improvement, seek opportunities for change, and implement them with measured adjustments.

The last agenda style is developer. Developers are committed to wide transformation and prefer to implement change through comprehensive and detailed planning. Simply put, these stakeholders are ambitious and want to overhaul. Unlike revolutionaries, developers do not improvise but rather plan and pursue change in a methodical manner. Their developer agenda combines the preference for far-reaching fundamental change with detailed, comprehensive planning.

Kathy Giusti, founder and CEO of the Multiple Myeloma Research Foundation, is undoubtedly a developer. Giusti founded MMRF in 1998 after she was diagnosed with multiple myeloma, a rare, life-threatening blood cancer. A seasoned pharmaceutical executive, she used her business savvy to lead the search for a cure.

Giusti analyzed the situation and discovered that the rarity of the disease was a disincentive for pharmaceutical research and that the few scientists who researched the condition were not in the habit of collaborating and sharing information. Knowing that she could never make a pharmaceutical firm-size investment in research, she turned her attention to working directly with scientists, research institutions, and diagnosed individuals. Her good idea was to use incentive-based collaboration as a means of finding a cure. The foundation "has helped introduce ten new drugs and through the power of new technology, genomics, and immunology, lives are now being saved."[33] One researcher noted that owing to Giusti's efforts, "myeloma now is a paradigm for new drug development, because of partnerships that occur between academics, large pharmaceutical companies, small biotech, the F.D.A., the National Cancer Institute, and foundations."[34] Giusti's detailed approach in executing her agenda has permitted MMRF to achieve great success.

Understanding the core agendas of others is fundamental to breaking inertia and overcoming resistance. What motivates them in the context of the organization? Where do they stand regarding forward movement? Politically competent leaders appreciate that individuals, groups, and business are different and have different interests and intents. For every proposed innovation or change, every individual and group will have a point of view, and the challenge for politically competent leaders is to perceive where others are coming from. This is not necessarily an easy challenge. In a myopic setting governed by the blinder mind-set, it may be easy to assume that there are a fair number of individuals and groups with traditionalist or adjuster agendas. Tinkering at the fringes may seem to be the common approach to change in the context of a myopic organization. However, this may not be the case. Politically competent leaders either will seek out the small group of revolutionaries or developers or will refine their idea or innovation in an incremental manner so it can attract support from traditionalists and adjusters. As Krackhardt points out, to move radical ideas in a conservative context, campaigners may have to introduce new ideas at the periphery.

In a clunky setting, with diverse interests and businesses and loose coordination, there may not be a core agenda. R&D may be a dominant force for revolutionary ideas. Corporate HR may have a more traditionalist focus. The HR partners in R&D may be developers. Some sales and production staff may be adjusters. In a clunky setting, the challenge for the campaigner is to figure out which group or individuals are more likely to support their innovation or agenda.

## Overcome Resistance

In breaking inertia the challenge of the politically competent leader is not only to understand stakeholders' power and agendas, but also to appreciate their fears and hesitation. Resistance is subtle and takes the form of the social psychology of hesitation. In many organizations, resistance isn't necessarily a strong fortress, but it is a loose conglomeration of apprehensions and fears that the politically competent leaders need to deal with. The fears and hesitation that reinforce inertia are often embedded in the clunky and myopic tendencies of the sluggish organization. Politically competent leaders need to address these fears to get beyond inertia. Three common hesitations are *fear of failure, fear of the new,* and *fear of turf encroachment.*[35]

The fear of failure is summed up in the question "Suppose it doesn't work. Then what?" There is nothing worse than having an idea blow up, and the political shrapnel can be dangerous. Every politically competent leader knows that failure is an option. Jeff Bezos thought that selling books online might be a good idea, but he had no inkling of the success that was to come. Lee Iacocca, while he had confidence in himself and the team, was not guaranteed that the Mustang would be a success. Mark Cerney was not given a golden ticket that would make the PlayStation 4 a success.

The fear of failure is often accentuated most dramatically in organizations with myopic tendencies. In a myopic organization, with its entrenched mind-set and set patterns of doing business, inertia and hesitation are rooted in the fear of failure. In myopic settings, perhaps only a minority is willing to take on the challenge of standard practice. In dealing with the fear of failure, campaigners are honest about the risks, but also demonstrate that the potential for success is well within the range of reasonable probability. Furthermore, in trying to get buy-in, campaigners couch their ideas in the reality of others, and put in their ideas in terms that make the idea of immediate relevance. The combination of possible success and relevance may provide a sense of reassurance to those who are bothered by the fear of failure. In this sense, campaigners will not be able to help others overcome the fear of failure unless they frame their initiative in a defined and specific way. Campaigners temper their excitement and are careful not to let the drama and power of their idea make them promise more than they can actually deliver.

As with the fear of failure, the fear of the new is particularly pronounced in organizations with myopic tendencies. Habit, in myopic organizations, is a powerful motivator, and there is comfort in doing things in the same way. In a myopic setting, patterned behavior becomes institutionalized and repeated. When it is challenged, there is resistance: "This is not how we do things here." The fear of the new is more subtle than the fear of failure. To overcome the fear of failure, campaigners make their case based on the probability of success. To overcome the fear of the new, campaigners place a greater emphasis on social-psychological safety. They provide stakeholders with a sense that their current position, practices, and patterns of behavior, even during periods when change is initiated, will be taken into account, and where possible, integrated into the new way of doing things. For example, when putting in place a new business model, a new supply chain, a new HR practice or pushing a new product, it is essential that the campaigner not only deal with the risk of failure, but also make it clear that smooth, nondisruptive integration will be achieved.

Even if stakeholders are confident in the campaigner's ability to execute, resistance may come in the form of the fear of turf encroachment. This is especially evident in organizations with clunky tendencies. In clunky organizations where authority and power are diffuse, individuals or groups may be afraid of losing ground, power, or control to other forces. The introduction of new ideas can shift priorities and resources that may make some feel alienated, undervalued, or nervous. Far-reaching change initiatives make it difficult for people to protect hard-won turf. New ideas may jeopardize older forms of status and power. As new ideas surface, some cling to old power structures and vestiges of authority. They resist change for purely political reasons. For them, inertia is as comfortable as an old shoe.

In the context of complex organizations where turf is both an obstacle and a reality, to get the buy-in, campaigners deal with the fear of turf encroachment. As such, they understand that concern for keeping one's turf is rational. Therefore, it is not unreasonable in the world of streamlining that one may be a bit paranoid about what they'll lose when giving support to a new agenda. Campaigners take these concerns seriously and help others overcome the fear of turf encroachment by thinking of ways to preserve or augment the status and resources of key stakeholders while implementing the new agenda.

A classic example of how these three fears reinforce inertia is the case of Kodak. Kodak was mired in inertia partly due to the reluctance of its leaders to support the development of digital photography. For over one hundred years, the company was a leader in photography, bringing it from the portrait studio to a part of everyday life. Its film success cannot be understated. "At its peak, about 70 percent of the U.S. film market, consumer or otherwise, was locked up for Kodak, and the company had a strong international distribution as well."[36] However, its success came with the price of myopia, and its leaders were waylaid by the short-term trap of continuing to pursue and protect their valuable film business at the expense of anything that did not directly leverage it. Kodak executives feared and suppressed anything that threatened film. Digital photography was one such thing.

Kodak engineer Steve Sasson invented the first digital camera in 1975, which altered the landscape of photography forever.[37] For the first time, the need for film had been eliminated completely. However, Kodak's leaders were trapped by inertia and used the three fears to justify their inaction.

The fear of failure was triggered by the uncertainty surrounding the untested concept of digital photography. By not bothering to devote the resources to fully vet the technology, Kodak's leaders could take a "nothing to see here" stance. The novelty of taking a picture and viewing it on a screen and having the choice not to print was hard for Kodak leaders to understand, and it was doubtful that consumers would embrace the technology. The prototype was "a rather odd-looking collection of digital circuits that we desperately tried to convince ourselves was a portable camera."[38] It would take considerable time and resources to bring it to market—too many, in fact, to see the project fail, especially if the perfection of this technology was decades down the road.

Kodak's leaders were not willing to disrupt the industry and throw the market in chaos. They were experiencing the fear of the new. Kodak was easily the global leader in all things film, and digital photography would change that. Its leaders understood that continuing to advance digital technology virtually guaranteed the breakdown of the status quo. That said, their unwillingness to accept this challenge was driven by their fear of the new.

Kodak's leaders had been with the firm for years and were ensconced in their titles and positions, which revolved around the centrality of film in the organization. The new technology had the potential to endanger their status and roles, and this is where the paranoia of turf encroachment came into play. Seeking to protect their power and influence, they "regarded digital photography as the enemy, an evil juggernaut that would kill the chemical-based film and paper business that had fueled Kodak's sales and profits for decades."[39] Fearing the loss of status power, the leaders of Kodak's film operations rejected the opportunity to further its development.

The story of Kodak clearly illustrates how heightened fears are a possible response to an attempt to break inertia. Politically competent leaders are aware that their innovation idea or agenda may rock the boat, and they work to find a way to address and alleviate the fears that others may have. The fears must be dealt with when forming an innovation coalition. The inability to properly tackle fears can lead to the failure of the most promising innovations, and the eventual decline of even the greatest of organizations.

▲  ▲  ▲

To make sure that delivery and implementation occur, leaders need political competence. Politically competent leaders are campaigners. In either a clunky or a myopic setting, they are able to deliver and implement only if they gain the necessary support. If they are not able to get through the metaphorical eye of the needle, nothing will get done. Politically competent leaders have the pragmatic leadership skills to create a coalition mind-set that ensures focused collaboration. They anticipate the power and core agendas of stakeholders and deal with the hesitation and fears that are endemic to both clunky and myopic settings. For all their active discovery, exploration, and innovation, pragmatic leaders know that campaigning skills are essential to delivery. Without them, inertia will never be broken.

## SUSTAIN MOMENTUM

In breaking inertia, pragmatic leaders may explore for ideas, move them to prototype, and gain support for those ideas. The remaining challenge is to sustain forward momentum and implement and execute. Just as leaders think that they have cleared the obstacles generated by clunky and myopic tendencies, they may stumble in final implementation. To ensure this does not happen, managerially competent leaders sustain momentum. Indeed, the core challenge of management is about creating the synergy to move things forward and ensure that the ball is not dropped.

No matter how enthusiastic the initial support, an organization's clunky or myopic tendencies may slow the project down. Sometimes initiatives fall apart, momentum dies, and execution fails because no one is quite sure who is in charge. This confusion may occur when the clunky tendency emerges and organizations make uncoordinated efforts, have multiple businesses, or are plagued with turf issues. In an organization with myopic tendencies, projects may collapse because of legacy issues or because one group or one perspective dominates the implementation process. In either case, organizational structures and processes may restrict and constrain execution and implementation, leading to reduced enthusiasm, waning commitment, or increased resistance. Therefore, managerial competence, the ability to sustain forward movement and ensure execution and implementation, is essential.

Take Carly Fiorina and the merger of HP with Compaq.[40] About three years after becoming CEO of Hewlett-Packard, she laid out an ambitious growth agenda for HP that included a merger with Compaq Computer. Fiorina used her strong selling skills and her political competence to build initial support for the proposed merger. From spring 2002 through spring 2005, Fiorina tried to implement the merger, sustain momentum, and deliver. While she was able to campaign for support, her ability to sustain momentum ran into organizational roadblocks. Units were relatively unconnected, and some in the organization had a blinder mind-set.

The analysts who supported her—and the merger with Compaq—turned critical or, at best, neutral on the "New HP." Shareholders and the board were supportive early on, but their support waned quickly as momentum was not sustained. The company's stock price and earnings stagnated. Fiorina had promised growth through innovation, through efficiencies, and through synergies gained with customer relationships. But three years into the merger, HP hadn't reduced its costs in the personal computer business; it had some new products (but no major innovation); and it hadn't yet realized the synergies of its combined customer relationships. Results were mixed, and Fiorina's "vision" had neither the support nor the results she needed. The organizational momentum for the new agenda was not sustained. Fiorina lacked the necessary managerial competence to execute and implement her agenda. She could not sustain forward momentum.

She could not break inertia.

There are two obstacles that may hamper forward movement and project execution. The first obstacle is the nature of organizational structures and processes. There is the possibility that the organization may be too centralized, too structured, and too bureaucratic; or too decentralized, unstructured, and not bureaucratic enough. Either case could lead to administrative bottleneck, holding up execution. Or the work processes may be overly rigid and directed, or they may be undirected to the point where the focus is lost. Beyond the structural and process challenges to execution, the second obstacle arises when project execution doesn't progress as smoothly as anticipated, creating hesitancy, second thoughts, and opposition—which can erode initial commitment, slow down execution, and diminish momentum. Monitoring structures and processes and maintaining commitment and direction are essential to sustaining momentum and ensuring execution. Fiorina could not manage the organizational structures and processes that could achieve results or maintain the commitment of her initial supporters.

To sustain execution, managerially competent leaders need to resolve the two obstacles to forward movement and project execution. To overcome the challenges presented by the bottlenecks caused by organizational structures and processes, managerially competent leaders must decide how much control or autonomy should be accorded to units and individuals as they try to move initiatives ahead. To overcome the obstacles to execution brought about by hesitancy, second thoughts, and opposition, leaders must employ strategies to make sure that units and individuals maintain commitment and direction.

## Monitor for Tight and Loose Execution

In monitoring structures and processes to ensure execution, managerially competent leaders ask some very basic questions: How should individual units and people carry out the project? How should the organization be designed? Who should report to whom? How should resources be distributed? Managerially competent leaders grapple with these bread-and-butter questions.

Implementation and execution in complex organizations is often a question of control. Simply put, how closely will activities be monitored, and how much space will individuals and units be given to carry out the work? On one hand, tight management of execution assumes that quality and efficiency are best enhanced by tight structures and processes. On the other hand, loose management[41] of execution assumes that the lack of predictability and the presence of uncertainty require that individuals and units be given a maximum degree of autonomy so that they can manage the shifting situation.

Tight execution implies relying on traditional hierarchy, output measurements, method specification, and centralized decision making.[42] Tight execution is best used when exploiting available knowledge, using traditional resources, and moving toward recognizable solutions.[43] In contrast, successful loose execution relies on fluid organizational structures, flexible rules, dynamic knowledge exchange, and constant adaptability of tasks. Loose execution is best applied when there is a belief that quality and efficiency are dependent on new knowledge, unconventional resources, and previously unknown solutions.[44]

## Tight Execution

Tight execution occurs when organizational leaders regard close oversight, a predetermined direction, and accountability as critical to implementation. By maintaining formal lines of responsibility, tight control, with its high organizational bias, allows for efficiency and project completion. Deliverables are assigned, roles are defined, and authority is concentrated.

Samsung is a multinational in businesses ranging from electronics to heavy industry and insurance. Samsung radically changed its position from a cheap and low-quality electronics maker in the 1980s to the world's number one smartphone maker. Samsung has managed to lead in innovation while running a very hierarchical and tightly controlled organization, characterized by rigid departmentalization, narrow span of control, and bureaucracy. Leadership is directive with centralized decision making. Vertical control allows the company to make decisive and rapid changes. Tight control allows Samsung to execute on their product innovations as needed.

Tight control is a two-edged sword. On the one hand, tight control may create bureaucratic obstacles, sidetracking projects even when small adjustments need to be accommodated. On the other hand, the centralized nature of the tight model allows leaders to make quick decisions when necessary. For example, less than two weeks before the launch of a new Samsung Galaxy smartphone in 2012, "vice chairman Choi Gee-sung ordered half a million blue phone cases to be thrown away as the design, with thin, silver stripes, was unsatisfactory, according to a person familiar with the matter. After a number of tweaks, Choi approved the final design on a Sunday just 10 days before launch."[45]

Global retailer Walmart is also organized with a hierarchal structure with tight monitoring for execution. At the retailer, "new policies and strategies developed at Walmart's corporate headquarters are directly passed on to regional managers down to the store managers."[46] To respond rapidly to changing customer needs, Walmart's corporate office "has a sophisticated computer network that allows the Home Office to monitor daily activities at every store.... The Home Office controls each store's temperature and mandates what music will be played inside."[47]

Walmart has a defined hierarchy starting from in-store hourly workers, managers, and executives. Don Soderquist, former COO of Walmart, credits Walmart's sustained success to "the hypercentralized managerial control that flowed from the Bentonville, Ark., home office."[48] Both Samsung and Walmart use organizational structures for tight monitoring for execution, relying on a strict hierarchy that allows them quality control and rapid decision making.

Tight monitoring for execution also occurs through the specification of work processes—how the work is actually implemented and processed. Many modalities of work and process improvement, such as Six Sigma, are an effort to institute a methodology of execution that ensures consistent output through tight monitoring and careful evaluation of each step. In analyzing achievement and goal attainment, these process-improvement mechanisms are predicated on the assumption that the process of execution can be not only tightly delineated but also validated.[49]

Leaders who seek tight monitoring and a high degree of direction over the work that gets done often routinize work processes and reduce the autonomy of individuals. By routinizing work processes, leaders attempt to overcome inertia by ensuring that both the pace of production and quality standards are maintained. Progress is tracked, and every individual is held accountable for their specific responsibilities and goals.

Apple under Steve Jobs had a sense of where it wanted to move. To move projects ahead and make sure that his vision was executed, his leadership style often relied on tight monitoring of the organization's direction and goals. Adam Lashinsky references the "Rules of the Road" document that Apple produces for every project, which "details every milestone leading up to launch day"[50] and "has DRIs assigned for even the smallest items."[51] DRI "stands for 'Directly Responsible Individual,' and it is the person who will be called on the carpet if something isn't done right."[52] Essentially, the DRI system fosters efficiency and control—the appointed DRI takes sole ownership for a given deliverable. There is only one person calling the shots—and that person is responsible for a project's success or failure.

At Apple, "there is never any confusion as to who is responsible for what,"[53] as there is clear record of accountability for even the smallest task. By naming someone answerable to the success or failure of a specific deliverable, Jobs made sure that the DRI executed their role as effectively as possible. From leading the team charged with releasing the newest update of the company's iOS (the Apple mobile operating system), to transcribing meeting notes, the DRI system highlights efficiency and tight control. Additionally, the practice of having a DRI reinforces personal accountability. From the highest executive to the newest employee, the DRI is responsible for the assigned deliverable. To this day, the DRI system is emblematic of the extent to which Apple's leaders practice tight control for execution and implementation. The DRI protocol ensures that tight control, efficiency, and personal accountability are Apple norms.

While Apple is a design and manufacturing company, tight control can be implemented in the service industry to ensure consistency and quality of service. In the early 1980s, Accenture (then Andersen Consulting) had been growing its technology consulting services rapidly.[54]At the time, the organization took a unique approach to each project. The combined pressure for growth and for profitable projects drove Accenture's leadership to develop a standard consulting methodology in the 1980s, known as Method One, which established a standard approach for analyzing a client's information system. By applying Method One to each technology consulting engagement, the organization's leaders believed the firm would be able to deliver consistent service, streamline project management, and generate more profits.

Every employee and new hire was trained in the Method One technology. Although consulting work is far from a "routinized" work process—every client is different and every problem has its own quirks—Method One provided the organization and its consultants a language, approach, and process that allowed the firm to be both consistent and cost-effective. While Method One is criticized as being too "cookie-cutter" in its solutions, the consistent methodology permits the organization to achieve unprecedented growth profitably and with a consistent quality of service.

The Accenture example illustrates that execution and implementation through tight monitoring is not relegated only to industrial organizations but can be implemented in service settings. Indeed, the consulting industry has succeeded over the two decades by presenting new employees—smart college graduates—with specific processes and templates to use when interfacing with clients. The routinization of the consulting industry has allowed it to become scalable. That said, when trying to move ideas in organizations that operate in a controlled environment, sometimes contradictions emerge. For instance, flying commercial airplanes is largely routinized. Under unusual circumstances, however, such as during a storm or when a bird flies into the engine, necessitating a landing in the Hudson River, overreliance on routinization could cost lives. Routinization assumes that the work conditions will have a degree of consistency. Tight control is challenged when uncertainty becomes a leading factor and autonomy is necessary for immediate problem-solving. While tight control may enhance the work of the young consultant, it may put the seasoned pilot in a bind.

Tight execution promotes forward movement by coordination, responsibility, and accountability, at the expense of flexibility, making adjustments difficult. If things fail to go as planned, and no one has the confidence or ability to change the plan, then the agenda can veer dangerously off track. Projects change and goals shift. Sometimes individual team members are forced to make a split-second decision that can have implications down the road. Managerially competent leaders who rely on tight execution must not forget that flexibility may be required to keep abreast of day-to-day change.

**Loose Execution**

In the late 1980s and early 1990s, McDonald's demonstrated the power of loosening control by embracing teams and increasing autonomy to overcome inertia and sustain momentum.[55] By the 1980s, McDonald's exercised tight control over nearly every aspect of its operations, down to the consistent menu and the ridged edges of its ketchup packets. It was a shining example of the power of hierarchy and routinized work processes in promoting efficiency and consistency of product. Its leaders knew their strengths and stuck to them.

By the late 1980s, McDonald's ran into the problem of being overly tight. They were overrun by the myopic tendency of playing too safe. Their momentum faltered and inertia set in. They were no longer thriving. McDonald's restaurants around the world were consistent to a fault in that every outlet looked the same and the food tasted the same in Rome, New York, and Rome, Italy. The problem was that tastes and interests vary all over the world. McDonald's leaders felt that the company was sluggish under the existing operating structure.

McDonald's responded to diverse customer tastes by restructuring its franchise operations and regional restaurant management systems. The organization loosened its control allowing regional and local McDonald's restaurants to have more autonomy and flexibility regarding menu selection. Consequently, the McRib sandwich may not show up on the menu in locations where that type of sandwich is not likely to be a strong seller. Or a broader menu of salads might be supported in regions where there is more customer support for healthier lifestyles. Japan's Teriyaki McBurger would not likely find a market outside of the country or, perhaps, the region.

McDonald's move toward loose monitoring paid off. Same-store sales grew, and franchise operators became more satisfied and motivated. Over the long term, the loosening of the tight operational efficiency enabled the organization to sustain momentum, fostering the development and implementation of new innovations.

Leaders who emphasize loose execution to sustain momentum are not convinced that the answer is in tight structuring of the chain of command or in delineating and specifying the work processes of execution. Loose monitoring assumes that to sustain momentum, hierarchy must be eliminated or reduced while the autonomy of individual units is enhanced.

Organizations like the game production company Valve and W.L. Gore (the force behind Gore-Tex) are known for their flat organizational structure and unique reporting arrangements.[56] Technology writer Leo Kelion describes a work environment that seems near paradise: "Imagine a company where everyone is equal and managers don't exist. A place where employees sit where they want, choose what to work on and decide each other's pay. Then, once a year, everyone goes on holiday together. You have just imagined Valve."[57] It is an understatement that leaders of the gaming firm exercise extremely loose monitoring over the organization, and Valve's structure is flat to the extreme.

W.L. Gore has a latticework structure in which there are no traditional managers, only "leaders and sponsors"[58] who seek to ensure the success of an associate and leaders that arise based on skill and ability to build followership. The company's website maintains that communication "is seen as crucial to our success."[59] Associates are encouraged to contact their peers directly, and not filter requests through their peer's leader.[60] Quick and open communication facilitates problem-solving.

Loose monitoring facilitates problem-solving and innovation. Leaders who prefer loose monitoring believe that projects are best nurtured by enhancing the ability of team members to make decisions and encouraging autonomy. They want people to be confident in their ability to adjust the plan—or their reaction to changing circumstances—without being bogged down by inertia. The final expression of a loose monitoring for execution is fluid teams—agile teams whose emergence is defined by the specific challenge ahead rather than external prescription.

Valve works on the principle of problem-based, autonomous, and fluid teams, where anybody can work on any project in the organization without reporting to a manager. One employee explains how they work, "We form into teams based on need to complete a feature or complete a game, and then we disperse into new teams."[61]

Executing with a fluid team structure may reinforce the notion that those closest to a specific problem are best suited to making decisions to resolve the problem. Having fluid teams may enable the organizations to respond flexibly and appropriately to customer complaints, requests, or emerging needs, without losing the opportunity or the motivation that gets blocked by a more elaborate decision-making and operating structure.

Fluid team structures require a high degree of communication and collaboration to sustain momentum. Because knowledge and decision-making responsibility are not concentrated and not built into the structure, teams rely heavily on information sharing among group members to generate creative responses and to effectively deliver products and services. Fluid teams can reduce bureaucracy and react quickly to changes in the market.

Zappos, the online shoe and clothing store, under the leadership of Tony Hsieh, is at the forefront of fluid teams. The company moved from a more traditional structure to a system known as holacracy, "a manager-free operating structure that is composed, in theory, of equally privileged employees working in [often overlapping] task-specific circles."[62] The system, as described by Hsieh, "enables employees to act more like entrepreneurs and self-direct their work instead of reporting to a manager who tells them what to do."[63] Holacracy implementation lead at Zappos, John Bunch, elaborates, "And so, while there's not somebody telling you exactly what to do, you need to make sure that you're adding value to the organization."[64] Execution becomes much more reflective than reflexive.

The self-managed system demands more from employees. Before holacracy, Zappos had 150 managers, and now they have 350 "lead links" who work on specific problems with others who agree to be on their team.[65] While the number of people in quasi-leadership roles has ballooned, managerial authority has not been transmitted whole cloth to the lead links, but is "distributed."[66] Brian Robertson, who devised holacracy, clarifies the role of the lead link: "It is not the lead link's job to direct the team, or to take care of all the tensions felt by those in the circle. . . . As a lead link, you are not managing the people; you are representing the circle as a whole and its purpose within the broader environment of the organization."[67]

One feature of holacracy is that team members can come from anywhere in the organization. For instance, if the problem under consideration is HR related, not only will HR be represented on the team, but anyone who has an interest in the problem being worked on. When the problem is solved or the challenge overcome, the team dissolves, and team members move on to participate in other teams. In this sense, not only team membership but also team formation is fluid.

Zappos encountered clunky tendencies while making the transition to holacracy. Some Zappos employees complained of preferential treatment by lead links, and some managers found it difficult to make the move to the new system.[68] While holacracy offered a myriad of opportunities for creativity, it is unclear how efficient it is. One former employee panned holacracy as "a social experiment [that] created chaos and uncertainty."[69] Since the company-wide introduction of holacracy, 18 percent of Zappos employees took a buyout package.[70] That said, the system has its advocates. One satisfied staffer said, "My worst day at Zappos is still better than my best day anywhere else. . . . I can't imagine going back to traditional hierarchy anymore." Regardless of Zappos's high turnover, Hsieh continues to be confident that the implementation of a self-management system is right for Zappos, but he understands that holacracy is not for every organization.[71]

Although loose monitoring for execution promotes the ability to respond to the fast-changing uncertainties of today's projects, it isn't perfect. Leaders who subscribe to this approach tend to ignore the time-consuming realities of project execution and may have great trouble coordinating many autonomous units. Flexibility and adaptability are useful to an extent. However, being too flexible and making too many changes may hamper the ability to implement. Organizations run by leaders who prefer loose control may have difficulty getting projects off the ground because of their broad focus and adaptive tendencies. Problem-solving and having the freedom to stray from the well-trodden path may spark creativity, but it may not be enough to get the job done.

### Take the Middle Ground

For organizations to break inertia, leaders must know when tight or loose monitoring for execution is most appropriate. If monitoring is too tight, myopic tendencies may present themselves. Momentum may be stalled by the strict adherence to routinized work processes and the chain of command. If monitoring is too diffuse, with individual units and teams having too much autonomy, turf battles and clunkiness may impede momentum.

Breaking inertia is a matter of balance. Pragmatic leaders who break inertia make sure their organization can adapt to constant fluctuations in the environment. They have the managerial competence to balance tight and loose managerial control for execution to sustain and implement their agendas. As such, these leaders sustain momentum and generate the synergy necessary to execute what they set out to achieve.

Alfred Sloan, CEO of General Motors (1923–37) and later chairman (1937–56), understood the concept of balance. Historically, GM was a clunky amalgamation of small and often competing companies loosely managed. Confusion at GM was so rampant that "it was impossible to pinpoint the responsibility for a particular problem—that is, to know whom to fire."[72] Poor, diffuse management hampered the ability of GM's leaders to coordinate and execute operations. Momentum faltered, with delivery occurring only after great difficulty.

To gain control over the clunky organization and avoid its myopic tendencies, Sloan dreamed of balancing its existing looseness with structural tightness to improve management of project coordination and execution: "In 1920, [he] wrote a long report about the best way to organize General Motors"[73] that outlined its future multidivisional structure that operated with both tight and loose control. Tightness was fostered through a central management team responsible for GM's overall strategy and resource allocation. Looseness was retained by breaking the company into semiautonomous product divisions, "each operated by a chief executive responsible for the operations, marketing, and finance of their business unit,"[74] allowing leaders to easily gather the information required to coordinate operations and diagnose issues. Product division leaders had the formal authority to make most decisions pertaining to the operation of their units.

Sloan further promoted looseness through emphasis on group decision making. He rarely dictated action. While he presided over the decision-making process, he empowered his teams to act on their own: "Whenever possible, Sloan exerted . . . influence by persuasion rather than fiat."[75] To balance the looseness of semiautonomous teams, Sloan established cross-divisional committees to ensure tight, coordinated execution.

As CEO, Sloan's mastery in balancing loose and tight control is evidenced by GM's dominance over Ford Motor Company. Ford had strong myopic tendencies and was tightly managed. While Sloan cultivated the power of group decision making, CEO Henry Ford (1906–45) favored a "dictatorial-style of management—he had a hand in most major decisions at the company and is said to have even monitored employees' activities outside of work."[76]

As large and tightly controlled as Ford was, its centralization led to chaos and difficulty in delivery. Simply put, the lack of structure made it hard for managers to follow through on decisions made at the top. In the 1940s, Henry Ford ran the firm in nearly the same way he did during the 1920s. His unwillingness to adapt to the changing environment and his distrust of corporate structure led to the entrenchment of myopic tendencies that sapped momentum for project execution.

Ford's tight control led to the leakage of talent. Fed up with their inability to have a say, top managers simply left. Consequently, "many of the executives that left the Ford Motor Company were snapped up by Alfred Sloan at General Motors."[77] Ford failed to balance tight and loose control for execution. The dramatic loss of his organization's leadership to GM was the result of this failure, in contrast to Sloan's achievement in balancing loose and tight control.

While GM pioneered the successful balance of loose and tight, Apple is a contemporary organization that has a tendency toward tight structures, but has the unique ability to loosen control and act as a startup when necessary. Current CEO Tim Cook once told an analyst, "I don't want anyone to know our magic because I don't want anyone copying it."[78] What Cook calls "magic" could be this balance of control. Unlike the decentralization and autonomy prevalent among many thriving organizations, Steve Jobs relied on tight control for efficiency and accountability. That said, Apple sets its itself apart from competitors through its ability to loosen control when necessary.

Apple's experience with DRI, as discussed above, shows that it disproportionately relies on tight control. That said, Jobs appreciated that execution and implementation sometimes required autonomy, and allowed for looser managerial control when warranted. A leader who prided himself on having "the confidence to follow your heart, even when it leads you off the well-worn path,"[79] he understood that these traits were not always the best means of delivering all projects. Under certain circumstances, Steve Jobs knew when to loosen his managerial grip and grant certain project teams leeway to operate outside of Apple's normally tight oversight. Deadlines were frozen and budgets were relaxed. Simultaneously, the best employees from every function would be relieved of their current assignments and placed into the special teams responsible for the development of the new technology or initiative. At this point, "[the assigned] Apple managers and their employees almost behave like talented rich kids: they have access to unlimited resources to do interesting things."[80]

By suspending control temporarily, Apple replicates the relative freedom and autonomy of the company's original startup culture, limited only by the resources the organization is willing to invest. Apple's ability to impose—and release—control is key to the consistent success of its project teams. Jobs balanced tight and loose monitoring, allowing for nimble teams where project implementation and execution flourished. The ability to impose and release control factors into the consistent success of Apple's project teams.

Sloan and Jobs intuitively understood what Thomas Peters and Robert Waterman imply in the last chapter of the now-classic volume *In Search of Excellence.* To execute and achieve results, they balanced tight and loose monitoring for execution.[81] To accomplish this, they developed a degree of ambidexterity[82]—and carried two sets of tools at the same time, one to tighten the organization's clunky tendencies and the other to loosen its myopic tendencies.

## Maintain Commitment and Direction

While managing organizational structure and processes is essential for execution, it is just as critical that leaders focus on the continued commitment and focused direction of critical parties. Breaking inertia in clunky and myopic settings is not easy. When things get difficult and the sense of excitement and collective commitment frays because of complications, obstacles, and adjustments, the social-psychological contract, which is necessary for momentum to continue, may fade. The sense of collective and common purpose may lose steam, leading to the reemergence of clunky and myopic tendencies, as team members retreat to their comfort zone. In this context, the managerially competent leader maintains the vision and a sense of common purpose.

If leaders don't maintain the spirit that brought the group together, it will lose its cohesive nature and ability to sustain momentum. An example of lost momentum due to the inability to sustain commitment is NASA shortly after the 1986 Challenger disaster, in which seven crew members perished. Hearings were held, resources were mobilized, new evaluation processes were put in place, and a collective safety culture developed. There was a sense that something was getting done and that it would be sustained over time. This sense that something was going to get done came largely out of the vigorous sense of competency, purpose, and action that often comes with a collective sense of purpose. While there is excitement in the moment, down the road enthusiasm wanes. Without continuous maintenance by leadership, focus may be lost, alternatives emerge, outside pressures are exerted, and people become exhausted, which is exactly what happened at NASA. As the agency was pressured to go back into the business of "flying the shuttle," and as memory faded, the collective mind-set committed to safety slipped away. In 2003, the shuttle Columbia met the same fate as the Challenger.[83]

Maintaining the collective mind-set to sustain momentum and break inertia demands that managerially competent leaders continuously reinvigorate the social-psychological commitment to the common purpose and stay politically aware. Without this reinvigoration of commitment, it is inevitable that inertia will set in. Managerially competent leaders make sure that challenges or countercoalitions do not redirect the original intent of the project as it moves ahead. Without continuous reinvigoration of commitment and political awareness, the collective mind-set can be lost, projects get off track, and agendas flounder.

**Reinvigorate Commitment**
Sometimes sustaining momentum can be a challenge. Sometimes

progress is slow in coming and enthusiasm flags. Sometimes when moving an agenda, the wheels spin, and it is hard to get out of the rut. In this context, to sustain a coalition mind-set, leaders need to reinvigorate commitment to the vision. Managerially competent leaders know it is important to return to the vision periodically and remind their team about the long-term objective. The reinvigoration reminder reengages people emotionally and reestablishes their sense of purpose and sense of vision. It refamiliarizes them with the very things that got them involved in the initiative originally, things they may have forgotten.

Merck is a pharmaceutical multinational whose "shared vision and mission is to save and improve lives."[84] This is a common thread that ties the employees together. Everyone understands that the bottom line is the number of lives that the company touches and improves. The organization defines itself as an R&D firm developing innovative health solutions. In an environment where it can take up to ten years for a drug to come to market, it is easy for people to lose momentum. The challenge that Merck leaders face is ensuring that project commitment and effort are sustained despite slow movement, bureaucratic obstacles, and setbacks that are common in the pharmaceutical industry.

By offering such experiences as the Merck Fellowship for Global Health, Merck leaders continually return to the core message, reminding employees that the bottom line is developing medicines that will help people. The intent of the fellowship program is to both develop talent and reinvigorate the mission: "The program pairs the best minds from our company with nonprofit partner organizations around the world to provide meaningful and systematic improvements in health service delivery for people in the greatest need."[85] High-potential employees are selected to work in collaboration with an NGO for three months where they travel to some remote and underdeveloped location. Once there, they observe and work to mitigate the health challenges that people living in those communities face. Often, employees describe their time associated with this program as a challenging and life-changing experience, which helped them develop both professionally and personally, enhancing their commitment to the core mission.[86]

Vaughn Beals led a leveraged buyout of Harley-Davidson in 1981 and took over as CEO (1981–89). Harley-Davidson was on the brink of bankruptcy because of poor-quality motorcycles and aggressive competition from Japanese imports. Beals wanted to revitalize Harley-Davidson but had to introduce an austerity program, which meant laying off 40 percent of its workforce, freezing hires, and reducing pay across the company by 9 percent.[87] Beals formed a coalition with the remaining employees to pursue the turnaround strategy and maintained momentum by reinvigorating commitment through employee groups and empowerment.

Knowing that executing the turnaround agenda would be a hard road, Beals tried to sustain forward movement by reinvigorating the commitment and strengthening the affiliation that employees had with the company by tapping into their passion and pride for motorcycles and Harley-Davidson. Beals introduced the Harley Owners Group in 1982, which allowed employees to sponsor rallies and spend time with other Harley riders. Many employees were Harley-Davidson motorcycle owners, and it was common for them to "talk about their motorcycle more than almost anything."[88] Being a Harley employee in the rallies was considered a "badge of honor."[89] For these employees, continuing to work at Harley-Davidson and helping the brand succeed was a benefit that transcended their work identities.

Beals reinvigorated commitment with employee empowerment. Empowerment under Beals's leadership meant involving all employees, from the factory floor workers to managers and salaried employees, in the company's decision making. He sought to "dissolve the distinction between blue-collar and white-collar workers." Tom Gelb, the vice president of manufacturing said that "no changes were implemented until the people involved understood and accepted that change."[90] Workers also received eighty hours of training in topics ranging from statistical operator control, productivity, and leadership to ensure they had the capabilities to pursue concrete changes.

By reinvigorating commitment, Beals sustained the momentum that was necessary for a successful turnaround. Motorcycle quality improved, sales improved, and the company became profitable. In 1986, Harley-Davidson went public, and by 1990 its stock had grown tenfold. Beals's successor continues the trend of increased employee empowerment and inclusion in decision making.

Establishing an e-learning program—with its new technology and pedagogy—is a challenge in the university context. In the late 1990s, many elite universities in the United States tried to enter the e-learning market but faced obstacles and challenges. Many early efforts in this arena failed to bear fruit. The clunky nature of the university, with its multiple interests, multiple missions, multiple colleges and units, combined with its myopic focus on traditional values and business models, makes it difficult for practically any change agenda to be accepted. In the case of the radical idea of university-sponsored e-learning, the university's clunky and myopic tendencies brought out the conservative, if not resistant, nature of many mainstream faculty and administrators.

Despite the poor track record of its peer institutions, Cornell University trustees launched eCornell in 2000. The new enterprise attracted a wide range of smart people who were willing to buy into the good idea of Ivy League–provided online learning. Within a year, eCornell moved the idea forward with the development of twelve courses. While they gained traction, execution was slower than anticipated, and resistance mounted. The commitment and enthusiasm that the eCornell team had in the early days began to wane. In 2004 Chris Proulx was moved up from being a staff member to become CEO. His challenge was to reinvigorate the commitment. He engaged in a series of small but significant exercises to ensure that the ball would not be dropped.

Proulx knew that he had to reinvigorate their commitment, especially since the organization faced an uncertain future. One of his first moves was to make a motivational speech to the remaining employees. He produced a can of Dr. Pepper and made the point that eCornell was like the soft drink.[91] Like Dr. Pepper, eCornell wasn't the biggest moneymaker in its market, but it had a place and a role to play. Proulx went on to remark that Dr. Pepper had been around for a hundred years, as a niche player and number three in the soft-drink market. If eCornell could do as well, it would not be doing badly. Proulx's primary concern was to encourage a group who had been with the firm since its dot-com high and survived two rounds of layoffs, but with its profile in the market and at Cornell much reduced. The Dr. Pepper speech was Proulx's maiden effort to reinvigorate commitment and to dissuade the remnant from jumping ship.

Another lever that Proulx used to stimulate commitment was the Fish! management concept. Fish! presents leadership lessons from a Seattle fish market. The first rule is to "choose your attitude,"[92] which reminds employees they could choose to have a bad attitude, or they could choose to have a good attitude. This was big news to a staff who was living in a grim reality that unemployment could be around the corner. In a shared space used by employees, numerous fish cutouts hung from the ceiling to remind them of the lessons learned from Fish! The Fish! mentality was important for eCornell in moving forward. Staffers were encouraged to email suggestions for the person who best exhibited the "fish mentality," and the nominees were routinely singled out for recognition. This was a way for eCornell leadership to engage in reaffirmation and to "celebrate the small."[93] Looking back on the Fish! experience, one staffer remarked: "I think it is a monumental challenge to get people to stay with a vision, stick to it and be committed when there are so many opportunities to go in a different direction."[94] But something as small as paper-cutout fish hanging from a ceiling helped people reorient their attitude and truly reinvigorate the mission. Today eCornell boasts a thick catalog of credit and noncredit courses and offers over fifty certificate programs, in areas ranging from beekeeping to data-driven marketing.

The Merck, Harley-Davidson, and eCornell examples illustrate what leaders can do to reinvigorate commitment and enhance affiliation. Merck, a large clunky organization, returned to the core vision of health care to sustain the commitment of key actors during a long, cumbersome process of implementation. Harley-Davidson, by reinforcing brand pride and enhancing participation and empowerment, weathered a tough period. At eCornell, reinforcing the social-psychological bond through a series of exercises enhanced the establishment of a now-vibrant and substantial program of e-learning in a resistant university environment.

Execution becomes difficult during periods of inertia. Merck, a large clunky organization with a global reach, Harley-Davidson, an organization with a somewhat myopic tendency, and Cornell University, clunky in structure but myopic in values, demand leaders with the common sense and managerial competence to sustain commitment and affiliation. Without managerially competent leaders, the ball will be dropped, and momentum will be lost.

**Be Politically Aware**
There is always the danger that inertia may reemerge. If there is a bump—or too many bumps—in the road, there may be a degree of

retreat if people rethink their support for a given project, agenda, or initiative. If subgroups feel that their interests are not served, they may lose interest in the initiative or form a countercoalition or try a different path. In a clunky setting, old turf battles may resurface, and units may return to their own priorities and core business. Myopic organizations may prefer to revisit traditional practices rather than move ahead. To sustain momentum, managerially competent leaders need to be aware that others can still stand in their way and slow down progress or prevent implementation altogether. They ensure that the various factions working to implement the agenda do not become uninterested in the project or develop the interest to move in a different direction.

Many an organizational aspiration, innovation, and agenda have gone astray because leaders ignored the presence of countercoalitions or political challenges, only to find out too late that their agenda was derailed by a group who gave perfunctory initial support or subsequently backed an alternative solution to the challenge.

Even though things seem to be moving along, and the organization is hitting the benchmarks of progress for their initiative, innovation, or project, leaders need to be aware if there is churn or discontent below a smooth surface. In clunky organizations, with their many competing factions and autonomous units, countercoalitions may emerge, and clash with the agenda at hand.

Countercoalitions are opposed to the effort, will challenge it publicly, and will actively work against it. Countercoalitions have a collective interest in opposing and changing the way the agenda is being executed. Dealing with countercoalitions is a challenge for leaders. If countercoalitions are ignored, leaders run the risk of losing commitment and support from their core constituents. This is a primary lesson that Carly Fiorina learned.

In 1973, OPEC nations embargoed the United States, sending oil prices sky-high. The CEO of ExxonMobil responded by creating Exxon Enterprises Inc., or EEI, which was charged to find nonpetroleum sources of energy and to prepare for a post-oil economy. EEI hired M. Stanley Wittingham, a chemist and materials scientist, who led the team to develop the first rechargeable lithium ion battery. The technology was years away from the production of a full-on electric-only car, but there was enough there to do something with a hybrid vehicle. Toyota was interested in developing the technology with Exxon, and teams from the two units came up a "roomy, driveable hybrid" in 1981.[95] Just as the momentum of the hybrid electric car seemed unstoppable, it was killed, not only by political and economic issues, but also by leadership shifts at Exxon. Oil prices fell, and a new generation of oil executives and managers who were not as eager to jump on the alternative-energy bandwagon were gaining prominence. The new leaders effectively formed a powerful countercoalition against the forces for alternative energy. They were in favor of increasing oil and gas exploration. One of this new breed was Lee Raymond, executive vice president of EEI. Raymond "recommended closing many of EEI's ventures and selling others, eventually shuttering the subsidiary by the mid-1980s."[96]

Exxon's role in exploring sources for alternative energy and developing hybrid cars ended here. Raymond became CEO of Exxon in 1993, and continued to reject research forays into alternative sources of energy. When Raymond was asked about alternative energy in 2003, he dismissed it as "a complete waste of money,"[97] and proclaimed, "Oil and gas will be the dominant energy until at least the middle of the century."[98] The agenda of the countercoalition against alternative energy continues to resonate at Exxon. Toyota forged ahead with the development of a hybrid car. The Prius was introduced in 1997, sixteen years after the technology was tested in Japan in partnership with Exxon.[99]

Countercoalitions have also played a part in the history of GM. A legacy of GM's dominance in the auto industry is its entrenched network of internal suppliers, who were granted a monopoly on whatever specialized part they provided the company.[100] This system created a high degree of turf awareness, and the leaders of each silo jealously guarded their territory. The advent of GM's first electric car, the EV1, not only rewrote the rules of car manufacturing but also threatened the cozy arrangement that GM had with its subsidiaries.

While the traditional suppliers assumed that they would have a primary role in contributing to the success of the EV1, GM vice chairman Bob Schultz and vice president William Hoglund thought differently. Knowing that the EV1 required outside-the-box thinking to develop the advanced components necessary, they enlisted a senior engineer from recently acquired Hughes Aircraft to work on the power train. The internal providers (known as the Delcos) didn't "like dealing Hughes in at all; they felt they could handle the power-train on their own. . . . They also felt threatened; perhaps the world's premier aerospace company would try to scoop up all of GM's automotive electronics."[101]

As a reaction, the leaders of Delco Remy and Delco Electronics, Bill Wylam and Al Lubenstein, joined forces to create a countercoalition dedicated to limiting the participation of Hughes Aircraft in the EV1 project. Schultz and Hoglund brokered an uneasy peace, insisting that Hughes work on the inverters but using parts supplied by Delco Electronics, and Delco Remy "would do the car's batteries and motor, and it could keep the smaller 12-volt inverter, but no more."[102]

There were continued squabbles with the development of the new technologies associated with the EV1, and the car made it to the finish line in January 1996. In 2003, the EV1 was scrapped, not only because of high production costs but also because of unresolved turf issues.

The countercoalition that emerged against Exxon's search for alternative energy solutions stalled the development of the electric car. Toyota was able to salvage some of the pieces of the technology, but it took years for a viable electric car to hit the road. Similarly, GM's inability to trim the wings of powerful suppliers also damaged the potential of the EV1. Leaders at Exxon and GM—who had the initial good idea—were not able to overcome the forces of resistance that actively lobbied against them.

Managerially competent leaders are alert to the possibility of countercoalitions and actively think of ways to tamp down their influence—whether by cautiously incorporating them into their coalition or by ignoring them and shutting them out of the process as much as possible. Coalitions are fragile, and managerially competent leaders keep them protected if necessary, and do their best to shield them from the slings and arrows of opposition, at least until the idea has enough staying power to enter the political arena on its own.

▲   ▲   ▲

This section dealt with some of the core managerial challenges pragmatic leaders face in delivery and implementation. Once leaders have new insights, develop concrete agendas, and gain political support for their intentions and direction, they cannot ignore the challenge of inertia that they may face when trying to implement and move their ideas forward. Managerially competent leaders focus on what they need to do to ensure that inertia does not reemerge and their ideas don't fade away. Managerial competence is the leadership capacity to sustain momentum and drive for implementation.

Managing for momentum is not easy given the constraints of a clunky organization, with its tendency to inhibit forward movement due to its multiple layers of turf and mixed agendas. In a myopic organization, leaders may think they have all the support in the world, but they can still be blindsided by the emergence of a countercoalition. Dealing with a serious countercoalition may set the agenda back, no matter how much forward movement has been made.

The managerial competence of pragmatic leaders is essential to breaking inertia. First, they make sure organizational structures and processes facilitate execution. They deeply appreciate the differences and nuances between tight and loose monitoring for execution. Given the right circumstances, managerially competent leaders are cleverly agile, and know when to apply one type of monitoring over the other.

Having managed the structure and process obstacles to execution, managerially competent leaders sustain the commitment and affiliation of key supporters and participants. Executing an agenda is challenging. In organizations with clunky and/or myopic tendencies, these challenges are even greater. Pragmatic leaders must continually make sure that the collective sense of a coalition mind-set does not dissipate, and they are attuned to the potential political opposition that may slow down momentum.

# CONCLUSION

## Pragmatic Leadership and the Couch-Potato Organization

**As discussed in this book, organizations get sluggish.** They drift into inertia, and some find themselves sitting on the metaphorical couch. Pragmatic leaders understand that couch-potato organizations never survive. Through their actions, they make sure that the organization does not wallow in past glories and achievements. Assuming that things will be all right is a luxury that, perhaps, existed in the past. In today's world, where organizations disappear as quickly as they emerge, the primary challenge of leadership is to stay ahead of the game and make sure that inertia does not become a way of life.

How long can you as a member of the leadership team afford to stay on the couch?

The reality is that organizational success depends on the pragmatic actions taken by organizational leadership. Pragmatic leadership is about the practical skills of execution. It's not about a leader's charisma, grandiose aspirations, or charm. It's about the simple and clear things that leaders need to do to move their organization ahead. It's about what leaders do, not about who they are. It's about the specific actions that leaders take to make sure that the organization is constantly moving ahead, taking on new challenges, forging new directions, changing and adapting. In today's world, with its volatility, fast pace in all sectors, competition, and urgency, organizations can be marginalized much more quickly than in the past.

Pragmatic leaders take on the two fundamental sources of organizational inertia—the tendency to be clunky or the tendency to be myopic. Clunkiness means being caught in perpetual organized anarchy, with relatively uncoordinated structures, overlapping expectations, intersecting businesses, and a general lack of focus. Myopia is a function of relying on old business models, being unable to be agile and adapt, being trapped by a blinder mind-set that prevents risk-taking, and being slow to overcome challenges. The clunky organization is sluggish because of structural chaos, and the myopic organization is trapped because of cognitive dissonance and the need to rationalize why certain things should not occur. Pragmatic leaders take on the challenge of inertia that is brought on by clunky or myopic tendencies.

In this context, inertia is broken and organizational potential is reached when leaders can stimulate robust discovery and focused delivery. Organizations can break inertia when their leaders are capable of exploring their environment, reading the signals, networking, making sense of possible directions, and then building on these cues to ensure that their organization can innovate and move insights into concrete new policies and prototypes.

To assure robust discovery, leaders must master the *contextual competence of explorers* and the *ideational competence of innovators*. To explore, they must scan the environment for useful information, read signals, and create partnerships. Leaders who are explorers make sense of signals, follow trends, and discover new ideas. Leaders who are innovators take steps to move an idea to germination. Innovators foster information flow, frame the challenge, lead for ideation, and maintain hot group culture. While explorers sense and initiate new ideas, challenges, and opportunities, innovators make sure that the ground is fertile and that the good ideas are supported by the resources they need to blossom.

Robust discovery is not enough. Pragmatic leaders must overcome the inertia of an organization's clunky or myopic tendencies so they can actually deliver. To engage in focused delivery, leaders must have the political competence to overcome the headwinds of resistance that sabotage forward movement and have the managerial competence to overcome challenges that could lead to dropping the ball.

To assure focused delivery, pragmatic leaders must master the *political competence of campaigners* and the *managerial competence of sustainers*. Politically competent campaigners create a coalition mindset, anticipate the agendas of others, and deal with the hesitations and fears of resistance. Campaigning is about the one-on-one contact that leaders have with stakeholders to gain support for their agenda or good idea. As is too often the case, good ideas do not guarantee stakeholder support. Entrenched interests, stuck cultures, and old commitments can result in the type of inertia that can be overcome only by leaders who have political competence.

No matter how great the idea, how wonderful the insight, how promising the innovation, or how deep the support, when positive momentum is not sustained, inertia reemerges. To ensure that this does not happen, managerially competent leaders sustain momentum by putting in place the structures and processes that balance control and autonomy and maintain the appropriate commitment and direction. They are fully aware that nothing is accomplished until it's implemented, and thus are perpetually focused on the political and managerial challenges that may undermine forward momentum.

This book presents a road map for breaking inertia within your organization and transforming it. Keep it close by on your desk or on the shelf as a call to action. The future of your organization depends on it.

## PRAGMATIC LEADERSHIP SKILLS FOR BREAKING INERTIA

| Contextual competence | Ideational competence | Political competence | Managerial competence |
| --- | --- | --- | --- |
| • Scan for information<br>• Read weak and strong signals<br>• Partner for direction and execution | • Structure information flow<br>• Frame the challenge<br>• Lead for ideation<br>• Maintain hot group culture | • Create a coalition mind-set<br>• Anticipate where stakeholders are coming from<br>• Overcome resistance | • Monitor for tight and loose execution<br>• Maintain commitment and direction |

Moving an idea, plan, or process in an organization takes the skills of pragmatic leadership. Without pragmatic leaders, clunky and myopic organizations will remain on the couch, wallowing in their past glories and living in inertia.

In the context of this volume, leadership is not simply a charismatic halo or an exalted vision. Leadership is the consistent behavioral and tactical action that ensures that organizations engage in continuous discovery and delivery that abates inertia. Pragmatic leaders lead their organizations by understanding five challenges of breaking inertia:

## THE FIVE CHALLENGES OF BREAKING INERTIA

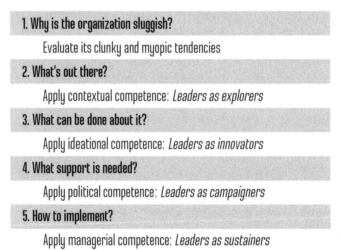

**1. Why is the organization sluggish?**

Evaluate its clunky and myopic tendencies

**2. What's out there?**

Apply contextual competence: *Leaders as explorers*

**3. What can be done about it?**

Apply ideational competence: *Leaders as innovators*

**4. What support is needed?**

Apply political competence: *Leaders as campaigners*

**5. How to implement?**

Apply managerial competence: *Leaders as sustainers*

## THE CHALLENGE OF INERTIA

There are two sources of inertia: the clunky tendency and the myopic tendency. The following questions will help leaders start thinking about inertia in the context of their organization.

Assess the organization's clunky tendencies:
1. Are the business units integrated?
2. Are the decision-making lines of authority clear?
3. Is there goal ambiguity or a lack of goal alignment?
4. Do competing agendas lead to turf and silo issues?

Assess the organization's myopic tendencies:
1. Does the organization have an overly rigid core mission and mind-set?
2. Is there centralized control of organizational mission and processes?
3. Is it difficult to convince others to explore new directions, new opportunities?
4. Is there a risk-averse mind-set?
5. Has the organization found itself lodged in one of the blinder traps?

## LEAD FOR FOCUSED DISCOVERY

### What's Out There? Apply Contextual Competence: Leaders as Explorers

Leaders who have contextual competence are explorers. The following questions will help leaders think about their role as an explorer.
1. Do you engage in both passive and active scanning?
2. Do you find that one type of scanning is more important than the other?
3. Do you monitor both weak and strong signals?
4. Do you create partnerships with customers, vendors, and suppliers? What are the benefits of creating partnerships?

## What Can Be Done about It? Apply Ideational Competence: Leaders as Innovators

Leaders who have ideational competence are innovators. The following questions will help leaders think about their role as an innovator.

1. Do you facilitate channels of communication, allowing for the free sharing of information?
2. In framing challenges, do you know when to use a small canvas and/or a large canvas?
3. Do you lead for divergence, convergence, and prototype development?
4. Do you maintain a hot group culture?

## LEAD FOR FOCUSED DELIVERY

### What Support Is Needed? Apply Political Competence: Leaders as Campaigners

Leaders with political competence are campaigners. The following questions will help leaders think about their role as a campaigner.

1. Do you create a coalition mind-set?
2. Do you evaluate which stakeholders you need/don't need on your side to implement your ideas?
3. Do you differentiate the core agenda styles of various stakeholders?
4. Do you help others overcome their hesitation?

### How to Execute? Apply Managerial Competence: Leaders as Sustainers

Leaders with managerial competence are sustainers. The following questions will help leaders think about their role as a sustainer.

1. Do you evaluate the advantages/disadvantages of tight execution? Loose execution?
2. Do you take a balanced approach to execution?
3. Do you reinvigorate the commitment and revisit the vision?
4. Do you anticipate the emergence of countercoalitions?

# Notes

## 1. THE CHALLENGE OF INERTIA

1. Jeffrey Pfeffer, *New Directions for Organization Theory* (New York: Oxford University Press, 1997), 163.

2. Michael D. Cohen, James G. March, and Johan P. Olsen, "A Garbage Can Model of Organizational Choice," *Administrative Science Quarterly* 17, no. 1 (1972): 2.

3. Charles E. Lindblom, "The Science of 'Muddling Through,'" *Public Administration Review* 19 (1959): 79–88.

4. Ronald Burt, "Structural Holes vs. Network Closure as Social Capital," in *Social Capital: Theory and Research*, ed. N. Lin, K.S. Cook, and R.S. Burt (New York: Aldine de Gruyter, 2001), 31.

5. Ibid., 34–35.

6. Ben Worthen, "Seeking Growth, Cisco Reroutes Decisions," *Wall Street Journal*, August 6, 2009, accessed May 9, 2016, http://www.wsj.com/articles/SB124950454834408861.

7. Ibid.

8. Therese Poletti, "Cisco Should Ditch the Committee Structure," *MarketWatch*, April 14, 2011, accessed May 9, 2016, http://www.marketwatch.com/story/cisco-should-ditch-committee-structure-2011-04-13.

9. Worthen, "Cisco Reroutes Decisions."

10. Pascal Vishée, "The Globally Effective Enterprise," *McKinsey Quarterly*, April 2015, accessed January 24, 2017, http://www.mckinsey.com/business-functions/organization/our-insights/the-globally-effective-enterprise.

11. Starbucks Company Timeline, Starbucks Corporation, 2015, accessed July 18, 2016, http://www.starbucks.com/about-us/company-information/starbucks-company-timeline.

12. John Quelch, "How Starbucks' Growth Destroyed Brand Value," *Harvard Business Review*, July 2, 2008, accessed December 12, 2017, https://hbr.org/2008/07/how-starbucks-growth-destroyed.

13. Tanza Loudenback, "The Incredible Rags-to-Riches Story of Starbucks Billionaire Howard Schultz," *Business Insider India*, October 21, 2015, accessed June 30, 2016, http://www.businessinsider.com/howard-schultz-profile-2015-10.

14. Aimee Groth, "19 Amazing Ways Howard Schultz Saved Starbucks," *Business*

*Insider*, June 19, 2011, accessed August 24, 2017, http://www.businessinsider.com/howard-schultz-turned-starbucks-around-2011-6.

15. Shirley Halperin and Ed Christman, "Starbucks to Stop Selling CDs," *Billboard*, February 19, 2015, accessed September 21, 2017, http://www.billboard.com/articles/6479986/starbucks-stop-selling-music.

16. Groth, "19 Amazing Ways."

17. Loudenback, "Rags-to-Riches Story."

18. Jerry Ussem, "America's Most Admired Companies," *Fortune*, March 7, 2005, accessed July 8, 2016, http://archive.fortune.com/magazines/fortune/fortune_archive/2005/03/07/8253419/index.htm.

19. Frank Hornig, "*Spiegel* Interview with Michael Dell: 'We're Willing to Change Everything,'" *Spiegel Online*, May 23, 2007, accessed July 8, 2016, http://www.spiegel.de/international/business/spiegel-interview-with-michael-dell-we-re-willing-to-change-everything-a-484592.html.

20. Ibid.

21. George Lodorfos and Agyenim Boateng, "The Role of Culture in the Merger and Acquisition Process: Evidence from the European Chemical Industry," *Management Decision* 44, no. 10 (2006): 1407.

22. Lawrence Pines, "4 Cases Where M&A Strategy Failed for the Acquirers," *Investopedia*, June 18, 2016, accessed September 17, 2017, http://www.investopedia.com/articles/insights/061816/4-cases-when-ma-strategy-failed-acquirer-ebay-bac.asp.

23. Steven H. Appelbaum et al., "Anatomy of a Merger: Behavior of Organizational Factors and Processes throughout the Pre-During-Post-Stages (part 1)," *Management Decision* 38, no. 9 (2000): 650.

24. Louise Story and Julie Cresswell, "For Bank of America and Merrill, Love Was Blind," *New York Times*, February 7, 2009, accessed September 8, 2017, http://www.nytimes.com/2009/02/08/business/08split.html.

25. Kateri Zhu, "3 Failed Mergers and What They Reveal," *Axial*, January 23, 2014, accessed September 8, 2017, http://www.axial.net/forum/3-failed-mergers-and-what-they-reveal/.

26. John Aidan Byrne, "Bank of America Accused of 'Tarnishing' Merrill Lynch," *New York Post*, April 4, 2015, accessed October 11, 2017, http://nypost.com/2015/04/04/bank-of-america-accused-of-tarnishing-merrill-lynch/.

27. Thomas Lee, "Dysfunctional Symantec-Veritas Deal Sets New Low Bar for Mergers," *San Francisco Chronicle*, February 11, 2016, accessed September 8, 2017, http://www.sfchronicle.com/business/article/Dysfunctional-Symantec-Veritas-deal-sets-new-low-6824714.php.

28. "Three Lessons From Symantec-Veritas Merger," *The VAR Guy*, October 16, 2008, accessed September 8, 2017, http://thevarguy.com/var-guy/three-lessons-symantec-veritas-merger.

29. Jim Price, "6 Reasons Why So Many Acquisitions Fail," *Business Insider*, October 26, 2012, accessed August 24, 2017, http://www.businessinsider.com/why-acquisitions-fail-2012-10.

30. Pines, "Where M&A Strategy Failed."

31. Jeff Bertolucci, "Skype, eBay Divorce: What Went Wrong," *PC World*, September 1, 2009, accessed September 8, 2017, https://www.pcworld.com/article/171267/skype_ebay_divorce_what_went_wrong.html.

32. "Wii U Production Could End by March 2018, CEO Says—Reports," *Gamespot*, April 27, 2016, accessed June 10, 2016, http://www.gamespot.com/articles/wii-u-production-could-end-by-march-2018-ceo-says-/1100-6439266/.

33. Ibid.

34. Ibid.

35. Josh Sanburn, "5 Reasons Borders Went Out of Business," *Time*, July 19, 2011, accessed July 8, 2016, http://business.time.com/2011/07/19/5-reasons-borders-went-out-of-business-and-what-will-take-its-place/.

36. Matt Townsend, "Borders' Bezos Champagne Toast Marked Start of Chain's Demise," *Bloomberg Business*, July 19, 2011, accessed July 8, 2016, http://www.bloomberg.com/news/articles/2011-07-19/borders-champagne-toast-to-amazon-s-bezos-marked-start-of-chain-s-demise.

37. Ibid.

38. Sanburn, "5 Reasons."

39. L.E. Yelle, "The Learning Curve: Historical Review and Comprehensive Survey," *Decision Sciences* 10 (1979): 302–28.

40. Daniel A. Levinthal and James G. March, "The Myopia of Learning," in "Organizations, Decision Making and Strategy," special issue, *Strategic Management Journal* 14 (Winter 1993): 95–112.

41. Liisa Välikangas and Michael Gibbert, "Boundary-Setting Strategies for Escaping Innovation Traps," *MIT Sloan Management Review*, April 15, 2005, accessed May 10, 2016, http://sloanreview.mit.edu/article/boundarysetting-strategies-for-escaping-innovation-traps/, 58.

42. Jonathan Dornbush, "Nintendo Thought It Would Sell 100 Mill Wii U Units," *IGN News*, July 7, 2016, accessed July 8, 2016, http://www.ign.com/articles/2016/07/07/nintendo-thought-it-would-sell-100-million-wii-u-units.

43. Välikangas and Gibbert, "Boundary-Setting Strategies."

44. Maija Palmer, "Sony Buys Out Ericsson from Mobile Deal," *Financial Times*, October 27, 2011, accessed September 6, 2017, https://www.ft.com/content/d7c78210-0068-11e1-ba33-00144feabdc0.

45. Hiroko Tabuchi, "Sony's Bread and Butter? It's Not Electronics," *New York Times*, May 27, 2013, accessed September 6, 2017, http://www.nytimes.com/2013/05/28/business/global/sonys-bread-and-butter-its-not-electronics.html.

46. Paul Smith, "Sony Chief Kazuo Hirai Plans for Post-iPhone Era as VR Finally Takes Hold," *Financial Review*, April 8, 2017, accessed September 7, 2017, http://www.afr.com/technology/technology-companies/sony/sony-chief-kazuo-hirai-is-planning-for-the-postiphone-era-as-vr-finally-takes-hold-20170404-gvdcav.

47. Välikangas and Gibbert, "Boundary-Setting Strategies."

48. John Curran, "GE Capital: Jack Welch's Secret Weapon: GE Capital Services Powers GE's Earnings, Drives GE's Stock, and Scares the Hell Out of GE's Competitors," *Fortune*, November 10, 1997, accessed September 1, 2017, http://archive.fortune.com/magazines/fortune/fortune_archive/1997/11/10/233789/index.htm.

49. Ibid.

50. "Banking on De-banking," *Economist*, April 18, 2015, accessed September 1, 2017, https://www.economist.com/news/business/21648681-announcing-closure-ges-financial-arm-jeffrey-immelt-has-only-won-half-battle.

51. Steve Lohr, "G.E. Goes with What It Knows: Making Stuff," *New York Times*,

December 4, 2010, accessed October 14, 2017, http://www.nytimes.com/2010/12/05/business/05ge.html.

52. Jeff Immelt, "A Simpler, More Valuable GE," GE, April 10, 2015, accessed September 1, 2017, https://www.ge.com/stories/pivot.

53. Steve Lohr, "A Stagnant General Electric Will Replace the C.E.O. Who Transformed It," *New York Times*, June 12, 2017, accessed October 14, 2017, https://www.nytimes.com/2017/06/12/business/ge-immelt.html.

54. Steve Brachmann, "The Rise and Fall of the Company That Invented Digital Cameras," *IP Watchdog*, November 1, 2014, accessed May 9, 2016, http://www.ipwatchdog.com/2014/11/01/the-rise-and-fall-of-the-company-that-invented-digital-cameras.

55. Claudia H. Deutsch, "At Kodak, Some Old Things Are New Again," *New York Times*, May 2, 2008, accessed May 9, 2016, http://www.nytimes.com/2008/05/02/technology/02kodak.html.

56. Chunka Mui, "Will Nissan Follow in Kodak's Footsteps by Rejecting Driverless Cars?" *Money Street*, May 20, 2015, accessed May 9, 2016, http://www.themoneystreet.com/will-nissan-follow-in-kodaks-footsteps-by-rejecting-driverless-cars/.

57. Richard L. Brandt, "Birth of a Salesman," *Wall Street Journal*, October 15, 2011, accessed July 19, 2016, http://www.wsj.com/articles/SB10001424052970203914304576627102996831200.

58. Jeff Saingor, "You've Got Sales Tax," *American Prospect*, May 6, 2013, accessed May 10, 2016, http://prospect.org/article/youve-got-sales-tax.

59. Leadership Principles, Amazon, 2016, accessed July 20, 2016, https://www.amazon.jobs/principles.

60. JP Mangalindan, "How Amazon Is Muscling into Entertainment," *Fortune*, April 25, 2014, accessed May 10, 2016, http://fortune.com/2014/04/25/how-amazon-is-muscling-into-entertainment/.

61. Hal Gregerson, "The One Skill That Made Amazon's CEO Wildly Successful," *Forbes*, September 2015, accessed July 22, 2016, http://fortune.com/2015/09/17/amazon-founder-ceo-jeff-bezos-skills/.

62. Eugene Kim, "Amazon CEO Jeff Bezos Explains Why the Fire Phone Disaster Was Actually a Good Thing," *Business Insider*, May 18, 2016, accessed August 25, 2017, http://www.businessinsider.com/jeff-bezos-why-fire-phone-was-a-good-thing-2016-5.

63. Henry Blodget, "I Asked Jeff Bezos the Tough Questions," *Business Insider*, December 13, 2014, accessed May 10, 2016, http://www.businessinsider.com/amazons-jeff-bezos-on-profits-failure-succession-big-bets-2014-12.

64. Mark C. Crowley, "Not a Happy Accident: How Google Deliberately Designs Workplace Satisfaction," *Fast Company*, March 21, 2013, accessed July 20, 2016, http://www.fastcompany.com/3007268/where-are-they-now/not-happy-accident-how-google-deliberately-designs-workplace-satisfaction.

65. Larry Page, "G Is for Google," Alphabet, August 10, 2015, accessed October 11, 2017, https://abc.xyz/.

66. Harry McCracken, "The Invention of Alphabet Is the Ultimate Larry Page Move," *Fast Company*, August 10, 2015, accessed July 20, 2016, http://www.fastcompany.com/3049693/the-invention-of-alphabet-is-the-ultimate-larry-page-move.

67. Katie Benner, "Michael Dell's Dilemma," *Fortune*, June 13, 2011, accessed July 19, 2016, http://fortune.com/2011/06/13/michael-dells-dilemma/.

68. Frank Durda IV, "Goodbye Radio Shack," February 10, 2015, accessed July 21,

2016, http://nemesis.lonestar.org/tandy/radio_shack_farewell.html.

69. Miguel Bastillo, "RadioShack's Mobile Hurdle," *Wall Street Journal*, March 29, 2012, accessed July 21, 2016, http://www.wsj.com/articles/SB10001424052702304177104577309850944349314.

70. Klint Finley, "Sprint Has Officially Saved RadioShack from Extinction," *Wired*, March 31, 2015, accessed July 21, 2016, http://www.wired.com/2015/03/radioshack-bankrupcy-deal/.

71. Jon Bois, "A Eulogy for RadioShack," *SB Nation*, December 2, 2015, accessed July 21, 2016, http://www.sbnation.com/2014/11/26/7281129/radioshack-eulogy-stories.

72. "Jeff Bezos: The King of E-Commerce," *Entrepreneur*, October 10, 2008, accessed July 21, 2016, https://www.entrepreneur.com/article/197608.

73. Sam Shead, "Amazon's Biggest Outdoor Drone Testing Site Is a Field in the UK," *Business Insider*, July 8, 2016, accessed July 21, 2016, http://www.businessinsider.com/amazons-biggest-outdoor-drone-testing-site-is-a-field-in-the-uk-somewhere-2016-7.

74. Greg Satell, "A Look Back at Why Blockbuster Really Failed and Why It Didn't Have To," *Forbes*, September 5, 2014, accessed January 12, 2017, https://www.forbes.com/sites/gregsatell/2014/09/05/a-look-back-at-why-blockbuster-really-failed-and-why-it-didnt-have-to/.

75. Kurt Eichenwald, "Microsoft's Lost Decade," *Vanity Fair*, July 24, 2002, accessed September 13, 2017, https://www.vanityfair.com/news/business/2012/08/microsoft-lost-mojo-steve-ballmer.

76. Ibid.

77. Ibid.

78. John Battelle, "The 70 Percent Solution," *CNN Money*, December 1, 2005, accessed July 21, 2016, http://money.cnn.com/magazines/business2/business2_archive/2005/12/01/8364616/.

79. Ibid.

80. Ibid.

81. Jeff Dyer, Hal Gregerson, and Nathan Furr, "Decoding Tesla's Secret Formula," *Forbes*, August 19, 2015, accessed October 30, 2017, https://www.forbes.com/sites/innovatorsdna/2015/08/19/teslas-secret-formula/ #2cec56ec653c.

82. Ibid.

83. Ibid.

84. Larry Huston and Nabil Sakkals, "Connect and Develop: Inside Proctor and Gamble's New Model for Innovation," *Harvard Business Review*, March 2006, accessed January 12, 2017, https://hbr.org/2006/03/connect-and-develop-inside-procter-gambles-new-model-for-innovation.

85. Randall Lane, "John Sculley Just Gave His Most Detailed Account Ever of How Steve Jobs Got Fired from Apple," *Forbes*, September 13, 2013, accessed January 12, 2017, http://www.forbes.com/sites/randalllane/2013/09/09/john-sculley-just-gave-his-most-detailed-account-ever-of-how-steve-jobs-got-fired-from-apple/#5c1ccb1a10e9.

86. Ibid.

87. Ibid.

88. Ibid.

89. Michael Useem, "America's Best Leaders: Indra Nooyi, PepsiCo CEO," *US News & World Report*, November 19, 2008, accessed January 12, 2017, http://www.usnews.com/news/best-leaders/articles/2008/11/19/americas-best-leaders-indra-nooyi-pepsico-ceo.

90. Ibid.

91. Bill George and Jay W. Lynch, "How to Outsmart Activist Investors," *Harvard Business Review*, May 2014, accessed January 12, 2017, https://hbr.org/2014/05/how-to-outsmart-activist-investors.

92. Ibid.

93. Michal Lev-Ram, "Disney CEO Bob Iger's Empire of Tech," *Fortune*, December 29, 2014, accessed January 12, 2017, http://fortune.com/2014/12/29/disney-ceo-bob-iger-empire-of-tech/.

94. Ibid.

95. Ibid.

96. George Anders, "Jeff Bezos Reveals His No. 1 Leadership Secret," *Forbes*, April 4, 2012, accessed July 22, 2016, http://www.forbes.com/forbes/2012/0423/ceo-compensation-12-amazon-technology-jeff-bezos-gets-it.html.

97. Ibid.

98. Matt Buchanan, "How Steve Jobs Made the iPad Succeed When All Other Tablets Failed," *Wired*, November 2, 2013, accessed July 22, 2016, http://www.wired.com/2013/11/one-ipad-to-rule-them-all-all-those-who-dream-big-are-not-lost/.

99. Ibid.

100. Ibid.

101. Adam Lashinsky, "How Apple Works: Inside the World's Biggest Start-Up," *Fortune*, May 9, 2011, accessed December 12, 2017, http://fortune.com/2011/05/09/inside-apple/.

102. Ibid.

103. Ibid.

104. Ibid.

105. Romain Mosecot, "Steve at Work," *All about Steve Jobs*, March 7, 2012, accessed July 22, 2016, http://allaboutstevejobs.com/persona/steveatwork.php.

## 2. LEADING FOR ROBUST DISCOVERY

1. James Titcomb, "A Thorny Lesson from BlackBerry's Rise and Fall," *Telegraph*, July 10, 2016, accessed August 3, 2016, http://www.telegraph.co.uk/business/2016/07/10/a-thorny-lesson-from-blackberrys-sharp-rise-and-fall/.

2. Dan Farber, "Jobs: Today Apple Is Going to Reinvent the Phone," *ZDNet*, January 9, 2007, accessed August 3, 2016, http://www.zdnet.com/article/jobs-today-apple-is-going-to-reinvent-the-phone/.

3. Matthew Honan, "Apple Unveils the iPhone," *MacWorld*, January 9, 2007, accessed August 3, 2016, http://www.macworld.com/article/1054769/smartphones/iphone.html.

4. Jackie McNish and Sean Silcoff, "The Inside Story of How the iPhone Crippled BlackBerry," *Wall Street Journal*, May 22, 2015, accessed August 3, 2016, http://www.wsj.com/articles/behind-the-rise-and-fall-of-blackberry-1432311912.

5. Ibid.

6. Jesse Hicks, "Research, No Motion: How the Blackberry CEOs Lost an Empire," *Verge*, February 21, 2012, accessed October 23, 2017, https://www.theverge.com/2012/2/21/2789676/rim-blackberry-mike-lazaridis-jim-balsillie-lost-empire.

7. Peter Sims, "The Hero Returns: Steve Jobs' Real Genius," *Medium*, August 1, 2014, accessed August 5, 2016, https://medium.com/@petersimsie/the-hero-returns-steve-jobs-real-genius-54f17709077#.vdg6aoqc0.

8. Harry McCracken, "20 Ways Apple's Mac Changed Everything," *Time*, January 24, 2014, accessed August 4, 2016, http://techland.time.com/2014/01/24/mac-thirtieth-anniversary/.

9. Samuel Greengard, "What Did Steve Jobs Do for Computer Science?" *Communications of the ACM*, October 13, 2011, accessed August 4, 2016, http://cacm.acm.org/news/136161-what-did-steve-jobs-do-for-computer-science/.

10. George S. Day and Paul J.H. Schoemaker, *Peripheral Vision: Detecting the Weak Signals That Will Make or Break Your Company* (Boston: Harvard Business School Press, 2006).

11. Ibid., 50.

12. Ibid.

13. Ibid., 51.

14. Ibid.

15. Ibid., 54.

16. Jeffrey H. Dyer, Hal B. Gregersen, and Clayton M. Christensen, *The Innovator's DNA: Mastering the Five Skills of Disruptive Innovators* (Boston, MA: Harvard Business School Press, 2011), 123.

17. Day and Schoemaker, *Peripheral Vision*, 55.

18. Ibid.

19. Ibid., 57.

20. Ibid., 58.

21. Martha Feldman and James March, "Information in Organizations as Sign and Symbol," *Administrative Science Quarterly* 26, no. 2 (1981): 171.

22. Karl Weick, *Sensemaking in Organizations* (Thousand Oaks, CA: Sage, 1995), 11.

23. George Day and Paul J.H. Schoemaker, "Scanning the Periphery," *Harvard Business Review*, November 2005, accessed February 10, 2017, https://hbr.org/2005/11/scanning-the-periphery.

24. Jennifer Reingold, "PepsiCo CEO Was Right. Now What?" *Fortune*, June 5, 2015, accessed February 14, 2017, http://fortune.com/2015/06/05/pepsico-ceo-indra-nooyi/.

25. Ibid.

26. Ibid.

27. Top Global Brands, Pepsico, accessed February 14, 2017, http://www.pepsico.com/brands/brandexplorer.

28. Reingold, "PepsiCo CEO Was Right."

29. Leena Rao, "It Took a Year but Fitness Gadget Finally Launches," *Tech Crunch*, September 24, 2009, accessed February 14, 2017, https://techcrunch.com/2009/09/24/it-took-a-year-but-fitness-gadget-fitbit-finally-launches/.

30. David Bolton, "Wearable Fitness Is More Than Just Tracking Your Steps," *Arc*, June 25, 2015, accessed February 14, 2017, https://arc.applause.com/2015/06/25/wearable-fitness-technology-health-research/.

31. Tamara Straus, "Fit to Be Worn, Worn to Be Fit / Lululemon Appeals to the Yoga Set—and Its Imitators," *SFGate*, January 8, 2016, accessed February 20, 2017, http://www.sfgate.com/living/article/Fit-to-be-worn-Worn-to-be-fit-Lululemon-appeals-2507153.php.

32. PR Newswire, "2016 Yoga in America Study Conducted by Yoga Journal and Yoga

Alliance Reveals Growth and Benefits of the Practice," Yoga Alliance, January 13, 2016, accessed February 20, 2017, http://www.prnewswire.com/news-releases/2016-yoga-in-america-study-conducted-by-yoga-journal-and-yoga-alliance-reveals-growth-and-bene-fits-of-the-practice-300203418.html.

33. "Lululemon: Building the Brand from the Ground—Yoga Mat—Up," *Strategy*, January 13, 2003, accessed February 20, 2017, http://strategyonline.ca/2003/01/13/lulu-lemon-20030113/.

34. Meghan Gustashaw, "J. Crew Gets into the Activewear Game with Help from New Balance," *GQ*, February 1, 2017, accessed February 14, 2017, http://www.gq.com/story/jcrew-new-balance-activewear-men-2017.

35. Devin Leonard, "Songs in the Key of Steve: Steve Jobs May Have Just Created the First Great Legal Online Music Service," *Fortune*, May 12, 2003, accessed March 13, 2017, http://archive.fortune.com/magazines/fortune/fortune_archive/2003/05/12/342289/index.htm.

36. Steve Knopper, "iTunes' 10th Anniversary: How Steve Jobs Turned the Industry Upside Down," *Rolling Stone*, April 26, 2013, accessed March 13, 2017, http://www.rolling-stone.com/music/news/itunes-10th-anniversary-how-steve-jobs-turned-the-industry-up-side-down-20130426.

37. Nathan Ingraham, "iTunes Store at 10: How Apple Built a Digital Media Juggernaut," *Verge*, April 26, 2013, accessed March 13, 2017, http://www.theverge.com/2013/4/26/4265172/itunes-store-at-10-how-apple-built-a-digital-media-juggernaut.

38. Retroprincess, "Gameboy: Nintendo's Handheld Revolution," *Need to Consume*, August 1, 2015, accessed March 13, 2017, http://www.needtoconsume.com/gaming/game-boy-nintendos-handheld-revolution/.

39. Ibid.

40. Ibid.

41. "Sony Takes on Gameboy," *CNN Money*, May 13, 2003, accessed March 17, 2017, http://money.cnn.com/2003/05/13/technology/psp/.

42. C.K. Prahalad and Venkatram Ramaswamy, "Co-opting Customer Competence," *Harvard Business Review*, January–February 2000, accessed December 13, 2017, https://hbr.org/2000/01/co-opting-customer-competence.

43. Biana Boske, "Qwikster Is Dead," *Huffington Post*, December 10, 2011, accessed August 14, 2016, http://www.huffingtonpost.com/2011/10/10/qwikster-dead-netflix-kills_n_1003098.html.

44. James B. Stewart, "Netflix Looks Back on Its Near-Death Spiral," *New York Times*, April 26, 2013, accessed August 11, 2016, http://www.nytimes.com/2013/04/27/business/netflix-looks-back-on-its-near-death-spiral.html.

45. "Deutsche Post DHL Group Confirms Strategy 2020 Growth Targets: Stable Dividend Proposed," DHL, May 18, 2015, accessed September 26, 2017, http://www.dhl.com/en/press/releases/releases_2016/all/dpdhl_group_confirms_strategy_2020_growth_tar-gets_stable_dividend_proposed.html.

46. Christine Crandell, "Customer Co-Creation Is the Secret Sauce to Success," *Forbes*, June 10, 2016, accessed September 26, 2017, https://www.forbes.com/sites/christine-crandell/2016/06/10/customer_cocreation_secret_sauce/.

47. Roberto Baldwin, "Netflix Gambles on Big Data to Become the HBO of Stream-ing," *Wired*, November 29, 2012, accessed August 11, 2016, http://www.wired.com/2012/11/netflix-data-gamble/.

48. Todd Spangler, "Netflix Data Reveals Exactly When TV Shows Hook Viewers—and It's Not the Pilot," *Variety*, September 23, 2015, accessed October 11, 2017, http://variety.com/2015/digital/news/netflix-tv-show-data-viewer-episode-study-1201600746/.

49. Tom Vanderbilt, "The Science behind the Netflix Algorithms That Decide What You'll Watch Next," *Wired*, August 7, 2013, accessed October 11, 2017, https://www.wired.com/2013/08/qq_netflix-algorithm/.

50. Chuck Lucier, "Herb Kelleher: The Thought Leader Interview," *Strategy+Business*, June 1, 2004, accessed March 17, 2017, https://www.strategy-business.com/article/04212?gko=8cb4f.

51. Marc U. Douma et al., "Strategic Alliances: Managing the Dynamics of Fit," *Long Range Planning* 33, no. 4 (2000): 581.

52. Ibid.

53. David Sanger, "Motorola, Toshiba Plan a Link," *New York Times*, November 26, 1986, accessed September 26, 2017, http://www.nytimes.com/1986/11/26/business/company-news-motorola-toshiba-plan-a-link.html.

54. Joel Bleeke, "The Way to Win in Cross-Border Alliances," *Harvard Business Review*, December 1991, accessed September 26, 2017, https://hbr.org/1991/11/the-way-to-win-in-cross-border-alliances.

55. "Netflix Case Studies," Amazon Web Services, 2017, accessed October 11, 2017, https://aws.amazon.com/solutions/case-studies/netflix/.

56. Angel Gonzalez, "Amazon's Stand-Alone Video Offer Pressures Netflix, Its Own Client," *Seattle Times*, April 18, 2016, accessed September 9, 2017, http://www.seattletimes.com/business/amazon/amazons-stand-alone-video-offer-pressures-netflix-its-own-client/.

57. "Why Did Netflix Migrate to the AWS Cloud?" *Matillion*, accessed September 9, 2017, https://www.matillion.com/redshift/why-did-netflix-migrate-to-the-aws-cloud/.

58. Leena Rao, "Apple Pay Now Accounts for Three-Fourths of U.S. Contactless Payments," *Fortune*, July 26, 2016, accessed March 13, 2017, http://fortune.com/2016/07/26/apple-pay-contactless/.

59. Ibid.

60. "MasterCard Nearby Launched as Companion App for Apple Pay," PYMNTS.com, October 27, 2014, accessed March 13, 2017, http://www.pymnts.com/company-spotlight/2014/mastercard-nearby-launched-as-companion-app-for-apple-pay/.

61. James Anderson, "MasterCard Digital Enablement Service (MDES): Making Digital Payments Happen," MasterCard Newsroom, September 10, 2014, accessed March 13, 2017, http://newsroom.mastercard.com/2014/09/10/mastercard-digital-enablement-service-mdes-making-digital-payments-happen/.

62. Michael Guta, "Apple and IBM Collaboration Results in 100 iOS Enterprise Apps," *Real Time Communications*, December 31, 2015, accessed March 13, 2017, http://www.realtimecommunicationsworld.com/topics/realtimecommunicationsworld/articles/415378-apple-ibm-collaboration-results-100-ios-enterprise-apps.htm.

63. Ibid.

64. Sheizaf Rafaeli and Daphne R. Raban, "Information Sharing Online: A Research Challenge," *International Journal of Knowledge and Learning* 1, nos. 1/2 (2005): 63.

65. Jeff Dyer, Hal Gregerson, and Nathan Furr, "Decoding Tesla's Secret Formula," *Forbes*, August 19, 2015, accessed October 30, 2017, https://www.forbes.com/sites/innovatorsdna/2015/08/19/teslas-secret-formula/#7d6a2af9653c.

66. Ibid.

67. Adam Lashinsky, *Inside Apple* (London: John Murray), 65.

68. Napoleon Zapata, "Managing Momentum for Change in a Large Organization" (master's thesis, Cornell University, 2017), 43.

69. Greg Satell, "Culture Can Be a Trap—Here's How to Make It an Asset," *Forbes*, July 15, 2015, accessed September 26, 2017, https://www.forbes.com/sites/gregsatell/2015/07/18/culture-can-be-a-trap-heres-how-to-make-it-an-asset/#6022ca4e2bfd.

70. Martha Lagace, "Gerstner: Changing Culture at IBM—Lou Gerstner Discusses Changing the Culture at IBM," *Harvard Business School Working Knowledge*, December 9, 2002, accessed June 30, 2017, http://hbswk.hbs.edu/archive/3209.html.

71. Lisa DiCarlo, "How Lou Gerstner Got IBM to Dance," *Forbes*, November 11, 2002, accessed June 30, 2017, https://www.forbes.com/2002/11/11/cx_ld_1112gerstner.html.

72. Ibid.

73. Ibid.

74. "Lou Gerstner's Turnaround Tales at IBM," *Knowledge @ Wharton*, December 18, 2002, accessed June 30, 2017, http://knowledge.wharton.upenn.edu/article/lou-gerstners-turnaround-tales-at-ibm/.

75. Stan Phelps, "Culture Is King: Three Ways Adidas Is Striving to Build a Culture of Extraordinary," *Forbes*, April 15, 2015, accessed June 30, 2017, https://www.forbes.com/sites/stanphelps/2015/04/15/culture-is-king-three-ways-adidas-is-striving-to-build-a-culture-of-extraordinary/.

76. Stan Phelps, "Adidas Reinforces a New Culture of Innovation with the Introduction of Avenue A," *Forbes*, February 10, 2016, accessed June 30, 2017, https://www.forbes.com/sites/stanphelps/2016/02/10/adidas-reinforces-a-new-culture-of-innovation-with-the-introduction-of-avenue-a/.

77. Ibid.

78. Ibid.

79. Charlie Kautz, "A Culture of Innovation Is a Culture of Listening," *Gameplan A by Adidas*, September 22, 2015, accessed June 30, 2017, https://www.gameplan-a.com/2015/09/a-culture-of-innovation-is-a-culture-of-listening/.

80. Ibid.

81. Tom Hormby, "The Story behind the Sony Walkman," *Low End Mac*, August 13, 2013, accessed March 24, 2017, http://lowendmac.com/2013/the-story-behind-the-sony-walkman/.

82. Ibid.

83. Nathan Furr and Jeffrey H. Dyer, "Leading Your Team into the Unknown," *Harvard Business Review*, December 2014, accessed March 24, 2017, https://hbr.org/2014/12/leading-your-team-into-the-unknown.

84. Ibid.

85. Katie Marsal, "Former Apple Product Manager Recounts How Jobs Motivated First iPhone Team," *AppleInsider*, February 3, 2012, accessed September 14, 2017, http://appleinsider.com/articles/12/02/03/former_apple_product_manager_recounts_how_jobs_motivated_first_iphone_team.

86. Ibid.

87. Walter Isaacson, "The Real Leadership Lessons of Steve Jobs," *Harvard Business Review*, April 2012, accessed March 24, 2017, https://hbr.org/2012/04/the-real-leadership-lessons-of-steve-jobs.

88. Spencer Lanoue, "IDEO's 6 Step Human-Centered Design Process: How to Make Things People Want," *User Testing Blog*, July 9, 2015, accessed June 30, 2017, https://www.usertesting.com/blog/2015/07/09/how-ideo-uses-customer-insights-to-design-innovative-products-users-love/.

89. Bruce Nussbaum, "The Power of Design," *Bloomberg Businessweek*, May 17, 2004, accessed June 30, 2017, http://www.bloomberg.com/news/articles/2004-05-16/the-power-of-design.

90. Scott Davis, "The Worst Ideas for Achieving Innovation," *Forbes*, November 16, 2011, accessed March 24, 2017, https://www.forbes.com/sites/scottdavis/2011/11/16/the-worst-ideas-for-achieving-innovation/.

91. Robert Curedale, *Design Thinking Pocket Guide*, 2nd ed. (Topanga, CA: Design Community College, 2015), 56.

92. Dyer, Gregerson, and Furr, "Decoding Tesla's Secret Formula."

93. Veronique LaFargue, "How to Brainstorm Like a Googler," *Fast Company*, June 20, 2016, accessed June 30, 2017, https://www.fastcompany.com/3061059/how-to-brainstorm-like-a-googler.

94. Matt Buchanan, "How Steve Jobs Made the iPad When All Other Tablets Failed," *Wired*, November 2, 2013, accessed October 17, 2017, https://www.wired.com/2013/11/one-ipad-to-rule-them-all-all-those-who-dream-big-are-not-lost/.

95. Ibid.

96. Ibid.

97. Ibid.

98. Luc de Brabandere and Alan Iny, *Thinking in New Boxes* (New York: Random House, 2013), 115.

99. "Steve Jobs: Innovation Is Saying 'No' to 1,000 Things," *Zurb*, July 25, 2011, accessed March 24, 2017, http://zurb.com/article/744/steve-jobs-innovation-is-saying-no-to-1-0.

100. Ibid.

101. Thomas S. Bateman, "Problem-Solving Lessons from NASA," *Fast Company*, June 6, 2014, accessed October 11, 2017, https://www.fastcompany.com/3031498/problem-solving-lessons-from-nasa.

102. Bob Granath, "Members of Apollo 13 Team Reflect on 'NASA's Finest Hour,'" NASA, April 17, 2015, October 14, 2017, https://www.nasa.gov/content/members-of-apollo-13-team-reflect-on-nasas-finest-hour.

103. "'Houston, We've Had a Problem . . . ,'" NASA, July 8, 2009, accessed October 14, 2017, https://www.nasa.gov/mission_pages/apollo/missions/apollo13.html.

104. Jean Lipman-Blumen and Harold Leavitt, *Hot Groups* (New York: Oxford University Press, 1999), 3.

105. Ibid., 10.

106. Tom Kelley, *The Art of Innovation* (New York: Doubleday, 2001), 70–71.

107. Leo Kelion, "Valve: How Going Boss-Free Empowered the Games-Maker," *BBC News*, September 23, 2013, accessed October 11, 2017, http://www.bbc.com/news/technology-24205497.

108. Ibid.

109. Harold Leavitt and Jean Lipman-Blumen, "Hot Groups," *Harvard Business Review*, July–August 1995, accessed June 30, 2017, https://hbr.org/1995/07/hot-groups.

110. Jon Gertner, "True Innovation," *New York Times*, February 25, 2012, accessed September 13, 2017, http://www.nytimes.com/2012/02/26/opinion/sunday/innovation-and-the-bell-labs-miracle.html.

111. Ibid.

112. Ben Paynter, "To Boost Creativity, Ericsson Thinks inside the Box," *Fast Company*, April 16, 2013, accessed June 30, 2017, https://www.fastcompany.com/3004745/boost-internal-innovation-ericsson-thinks-inside-boxes.

113. Ibid.

114. Theo Priestley, "Why Every Business Should Run Internal Hackathons," *Forbes*, January 20, 2016, accessed March 17, 2017, https://www.forbes.com/sites/theopriestley/2016/01/20/why-every-business-should-run-internal-hackathons/.

115. Jennifer Elias, "Why Do Big Companies Do Hackathons?" *Fast Company*, May 14, 2014, accessed March 21, 2017, https://www.fastcompany.com/3030628/why-do-big-companies-do-hackathons.

116. Bouk de Ruijter, "Hackathon: Hacking into Digital Transformation," *Ditra*, February 5, 2016, accessed March 21, 2017, https://www.ditragroup.com/2016/02/05/hacking-into-digital-transformation/.

117. *Dice* staff, "How Hackathons Boost Tech Pro Hiring," *Dice*, February 16, 2017, accessed March 21, 2017, http://insights.dice.com/2017/02/16/hackathons-boost-tech-pro-hiring/.

118. Ferry Gripink, Alan Lau, and Javier Vara, "Demystifying the Hackathon," *McKinsey & Company: Digital McKinsey*, October 2015, accessed March 21, 2017, http://www.mckinsey.com/business-functions/digital-mckinsey/our-insights/demystifying-the-hackathon.

119. De Ruijter, "Hackathon."

120. Dave Fontenot, "WTF Is a Hackathon?" *Medium*, October 7, 2013, accessed March 21, 2017, https://medium.com/hackathons-anonymous/wtf-is-a-hackathon-92668579601.

121. Nicholas Carlson, "The Real History of Twitter," *Business Insider*, April 13, 2011, accessed September 13, 2017, http://www.businessinsider.com/how-twitter-was-founded-2011-4.

122. Ibid.

## 3. LEADING FOR FOCUSED DELIVERY

1. Samuel B. Bacharach, *The Agenda Mover: When Your Good Idea Is Not Enough* (Ithaca, NY: Cornell University Press, 2016), 162.

2. Shaul Oreg and Jacob Goldenburg, *Resistance to Innovation: Its Sources and Manifestations* (Chicago: Chicago University Press, 2015), 5.

3. David Krackhardt, "Viscosity Models and the Diffusion of Controversial Innovations," in *Dynamics of Organizations: Computational Modeling and Organization Theories*, ed. Alessandro Lomi and Erik R. Larsen (Cambridge, MA: MIT Press, 2001), 243–68, accessed October 11, 2017, http://www.andrew.cmu.edu/user/krack/documents/pubs/1997/1997%20Viscosity%20and%20C.

4. Ibid.

5. Kurt Eichenwald, "Microsoft's Lost Decade," *Vanity Fair*, July 24, 2002, accessed September 13, 2017, https://www.vanityfair.com/news/business/2012/08/microsoft-lost-mojo-steve-ballmer.

6. Ibid.

7. Ibid.

8. Ibid.

9. Ibid.

10. Cade Metz, "Exclusive: The American Who Remade the Playstation 4 and Remade Sony," *Wired*, November 7, 2013, accessed October 1, 2017, https://www.wired.com/2013/11/playstation-4/.

11. Ibid.

12. Ibid.

13. Ibid.

14. Ibid.

15. Paritosh Bansal, "Special Report: Inside AIG's Tortuous Turnaround," *Reuters*, December 21, 2010, accessed October 1, 2017, https://www.reuters.com/article/us-aig-ipo/special-report-inside-aigs-tortuous-turnaround-idUSTRE6BK3G020101221.

16. Jake DeSantis, "Dear A.I.G., I Quit!" *New York Times*, March 24, 2009, accessed October 1, 2017, http://www.nytimes.com/2009/03/25/opinion/25desantis.html.

17. Jessica Pressler, "The Randian and the Bailout," *New York Magazine*, October 21, 2012, accessed October 1, 2017, http://nymag.com/news/features/bob-benmosche-aig-2012-10/index3.html.

18. Jonathan Kandell, "Robert Benmosche, Rescuer of A.I.G. after Bailout, Dies at 70," *New York Times*, February 27, 2015, accessed October 1, 2017, https://www.nytimes.com/2015/02/28/business/dealbook/robert-benmosche-ex-metlife-chief-who-rescued-aig-dies-at-70.html.

19. Bacharach, *Agenda Mover*, 20–23.

20. Matt Anderson, "Mustang: The Birth of an American Icon," The Henry Ford, June 11, 2014, accessed April 10, 2017, https://www.thehenryford.org/explore/blog/mustang-the-birth-of-an-american-icon.

21. Ibid.

22. Ibid.

23. Bacharach, *Agenda Mover*, 32–33.

24. Samuel B. Bacharach, *Get Them on Your Side* (Avon, MA: Adams Media, 2005), 40.

25. Steve Lohr, "Technology: Main Opponent to Hewlett-Compaq Deal Goes Public," *New York Times*, February 1, 2002, accessed September 13, 2017, http://www.nytimes.com/2001/12/14/business/technology-hewlett-heir-issues-letter-denouncing-planned-deal.html.

26. Steve Lohr, "Endorsement for Hewlett Deal," Technology Briefing: Software, *New York Times*, January 29, 2002, accessed September 29, 2017, http://www.nytimes.com/2002/01/29/business/technology-briefing-software-endorsement-for-hewlett-deal.html.

27. Joel Siegel, "When Steve Jobs Got Fired by Apple," *ABC News*, October 6, 2011, accessed April 10, 2017, http://abcnews.go.com/Technology/steve-jobs-fire-company/story?id=14683754.

28. Randall Lane, "John Sculley Just Gave His Most Detailed Account Ever of How Steve Jobs Got Fired from Apple," *Forbes*, September 13, 2013, accessed April 10, 2017,

http://www.forbes.com/sites/randalllane/2013/09/09/john-sculley-just-gave-his-most-detailed-account-ever-of-how-steve-jobs-got-fired-from-apple/#5c1ccb1a10e9.

29. Ibid.

30. Adam Lashinsky, "Apple's Tim Cook Leads Different," *Fortune*, March 20, 2015, accessed September 13, 2017, http://fortune.com/2015/03/26/tim-cook/.

31. Rhiannon Williams, "The Timeline of How Apple Watch Was Created," *Business Insider*, March 9, 2015, accessed October 18, 2017, http://www.businessinsider.com/a-timeline-of-how-the-apple-watch-was-created-2015-3.

32. Brian X. Chen, "Apple to Pay $3 Billion to Buy Beats," *New York Times*, May 28, 2014, accessed October 18, 2017, https://www.nytimes.com/2014/05/29/technology/apple-confirms-its-3-billion-deal-for-beats-electronics.html.

33. "Learn the Basics about Multiple Myeloma," MMRF, accessed September 13, 2017, https://www.themmrf.org/multiple-myeloma/.

34. Jerome Groopman, "Buying a Cure," *New Yorker*, January 28, 2008, accessed October 3, 2017, https://www.newyorker.com/magazine/2008/01/28/buying-a-cure.

35. Bacharach, *Agenda Mover*, 101.

36. Steve Brachman, "The Rise and Fall of the Company That Invented Digital Cameras," *IPWatchdog*, November 1, 2014, accessed October 1, 2017, http://www.ipwatchdog.com/2014/11/01/the-rise-and-fall-of-the-company-that-invented-digital-cameras/.

37. Ibid.

38. Audley Jarvis, "How Kodak Invented the Digital Camera in 1975," *Techradar*, May 9, 2008, accessed October 1, 2017, http://www.techradar.com/news/cameras/photography-video-capture/how-kodak-invented-the-digital-camera-in-1975-364822.

39. Claudia H. Deutsch, "At Kodak, Some Old Things Are New Again," *New York Times*, May 2, 2008, accessed October 1, 2017, http://www.nytimes.com/2008/05/02/technology/02kodak.html.

40. Samuel B. Bacharach, *Keep Them on Your Side* (Avon, MA: Adams Media, 2006), 12–13.

41. Karl Weick, "Educational Organizations as Loosely Coupled Systems," *Administrative Science Quarterly* 21 (1976): 1–19.

42. Tom Burns and G.M. Stalker, *The Management of Innovation* (London: Tavistock, 1961).

43. James G. March, "Exploration and Exploitation in Organizational Learning," *Organization Science* 2, no. 1 (1991): 71–87.

44. Ibid.

45. Tim Worstall, "Apple v Samsung: Corporate Cultures and Design," *Forbes*, September 3, 2012, accessed October 28, 2017, https://www.forbes.com/sites/tim-worstall/2012/09/03/apple-v-samsung-corporate-cultures-and-design/#6cd02cb1d38c.

46. Jessica Lombard, "Walmart: Organizational Structure and Organizational Culture," Panmore Institute, January 27, 2017, accessed October 30, 2017, http://panmore.com/walmart-organizational-structure-organizational-culture.

47. "Wal-Mart's Centralized Corporate Control Spreads Gender Discrimination throughout the U.S.," *Justice Watch*, Alliance for Justice, March 26, 2011, accessed October 30, 2017, http://afjjusticewatch.blogspot.com/2011/03/wal-marts-centralized-corporate-control.html.

48. Nelson Lichtenstein, "Wal-Mart's Authoritarian Culture," *New York Times*, June 21, 2011, accessed October 30, 2017, http://www.nytimes.com/2011/06/22/opin-

ion/22Lichtenstein.html.

49. Rick Freedman, "Six Sigma: Changing Organizations for the Better," *Tech Republic*, July 20, 2009, accessed October 27, 2017, http://www.techrepublic.com/blog/tech-decision-maker/six-sigma-changing-organizations-for-the-better/.

50. Adam Lashinsky, *Inside Apple: How America's Most Admired—and Secretive—Company Really Works* (New York: Business Plus, 2013), 39.

51. Ibid., 68.

52. Ibid., 67.

53. Ibid., 68.

54. Bacharach, *Keep Them on Your Side*, 108–9.

55. Ibid., 93–94.

56. Jacob Morgan, "The 5 Types of Organizational Structures: Part 3; Flat Organizations," *Forbes*, July 13, 2015, accessed October 1, 2017, https://www.forbes.com/sites/jacobmorgan/2015/07/13/the-5-types-of-organizational-structures-part-3-flat-organizations/#4b305e7c6caa.

57. Leo Kelion, "Valve: How Going Boss-Free Empowered the Games-Maker," *BBC News*, September 23, 2013, accessed October 11, 2017, http://www.bbc.com/news/technology-24205497.

58. "Working at Gore," Gore, 2017, accessed October 11, 2017, https://www.gore.com/about/working-at-gore.

59. Ibid.

60. Ibid.

61. Kelion, "Valve."

62. Richard Feloni, "Inside Zappos CEO Tony Hsieh's Radical Management Experiment That Prompted 14% of Employees to Quit," *Business Insider*, May 16, 2015, accessed October 10, 2017, http://www.businessinsider.com/tony-hsieh-zappos-holacracy-management-experiment-2015-5.

63. Nicole Leinback-Reyhle, "Shedding Hierarchy: Could Zappos Be Setting an Innovative Trend?" *Forbes*, July 15, 2014, accessed October 10, 2017, https://www.forbes.com/sites/nicoleleinbachreyhle/2014/07/15/shedding-hierarchy-could-zappos-be-setting-an-innvoative-trend/.

64. Ethan Bernstein and John Bunch, "The Zappos Holacracy Experiment," *Harvard Business Review*, July 28, 2016, accessed October 10, 2017, https://hbr.org/ideacast/2016/07/the-zappos-holacracy-experiment.html.

65. Ibid.

66. Feloni, "Inside Zappos."

67. Richard Feloni, "Here's How the 'Self-Management' System That Zappos Is Using Actually Works," *Business Insider*, June 3, 2015, accessed December 13, 2017, http://www.businessinsider.com/how-zappos-self-management-system-holacracy-works-2015-6.

68. Jennifer Reingold, "How a Radical Shift Left Zappos Reeling," *Fortune*, March 4, 2015, accessed October 10, 2017, http://fortune.com/zappos-tony-hsieh-holacracy/.

69. Ibid.

70. Lauren French, "Zappos' Weird Management Style Is Costing It More Employees," *Time*, January 14, 2016, accessed October 10, 2017, http://time.com/4180791/zappos-holacracy-buyouts/.

71. Reingold, "Shift Left Zappos Reeling."

72. Thomas K. McCraw, *American Business since 1920: How It Worked*, 2nd ed.

(Chichester: Wiley/Blackwell, 2009), 28.

73. Jamie LaReau, "After the Frenetic Durant Era, Sloan Brought Order from Chaos," *Automotive News*, September 14, 2008, accessed October 15, 2017, http://www.autonews.com/article/20080914/oem02/309149952/.

74. Mario Vellandi, "Alfred Sloan and the Discipline of Organizational Management," *Journal-Mario Vellandi*, January 28, 2008, accessed October 15, 2017, https://mvellandi.gitbub.io/journal/alfred-sloan-and-organizational-management/.

75. McCraw, *American Business since 1920*, 29.

76. Amy Gunderson, "The Great Leaders Series: Henry Ford, Founder of Ford Motor Company," *Inc.*, November 4, 2009, accessed October 15, 2017, https://www.inc.com/30years/articles/henry-ford.html.

77. McCraw, *American Business since 1920*, 25.

78. Adam Lashinsky, "How Apple Works: Inside the World's Biggest Startup," *Fortune*, May 9, 2011, accessed July 22, 2016, http://fortune.com/2011/05/09/inside-apple/.

79. Steve Jobs, commencement address at Stanford University, Palo Alto, CA, June 5, 2005, American Rhetoric, accessed October 11, 2017, http://www.americanrhetoric.com/speeches/stevejobsstanfordcommencement.htm.

80. Lashinsky, *Inside Apple*, 69.

81. Thomas J. Peters and Robert H. Waterman Jr., *In Search of Excellence* (New York: Harper Collins, 2006), 318.

82. Charles A. O'Reilly III and Michael L. Tushman, *Lead and Disrupt: How to Solve the Innovator's Dilemma* (Stanford, CA: Stanford University Press, 2016); Tom J.M. Mom, Frans A.J. van den Bosch, and Henk W. Volberda, "Understanding Variation in Managers' Ambidexterity: Investigating Direct and Interaction Effects of Formal Structural and Personal Coordination Mechanisms," *Organization Science* 20, no. 4 (2009): 812–28.

83. Bacharach, *Keep Them on Your Side*, 182–83.

84. "About Us," Merck, accessed July 17, 2017, http://www.merck.com/about/home.html.

85. "MSD Fellowship For Global Health," Merck & Co., Inc., accessed January 16, 2018, https://www.msdresponsibility.com/our-giving/msd-fellowship-for-global-health/.

86. Napoleon Zapata, "Managing Momentum for Change in a Large Organization" (master's thesis, Cornell University, 2017), 37.

87. Rich Teerlink, "Harley's Leadership U-Turn," *Harvard Business Review*, July–August 2000, accessed October 11, 2017, https://hbr.org/2000/07/harleys-leadership-u-turn.

88. Daniel Gross, "The Turnaround at Harley-Davidson," *Forbes*, August 21, 1997, accessed October 6, 2017, http://www.uic.edu.hk/~kentsang/powerst/forbes-The%20Turnaround%20at%20Harley-Davidson.pdf.

89. Glenn Rifkin, "How Harley Davidson Revs Its Brand," *Strategy+Business*, October 1, 1997, accessed October 6, 2017, https://www.strategy-business.com/article/12878.

90. Daniel Gross, "The Turnaround at Harley-Davidson," *Forbes*, August 21, 1997, accessed October 6, 2017, http://www.uic.edu.hk/~kentsang/powerst/forbes-The%20Turnaround%20at%20Harley-Davidson.pdf.

91. Chris Proulx, class lecture, ILROB 525, Cornell University, Ithaca, NY, March 1, 2008.

92. Stephen C. Lundin, Harry Paul, and John Christensen, *Fish! A Remarkable Way to Boost Morale and Improve Results* (New York: Hyperion, 2000), 37.

93. Proulx, class lecture.

94. Tom Abogabal, interviewed by the author, June 9, 2008.

95. Neela Banerjee, "For Exxon, Hybrid Car Technology Was Another Road Not Taken," *Inside Climate News*, October 5, 2016, accessed October 11, 2017, https://inside-climatenews.org/news/04102016/exxon-climate-change-hybrid-cars-technology-another-road-not-taken-electric-vehicle-toyota-prius.

96. Ibid.

97. "The Unrepentant Oilman," *Economist*, March 13, 2003, accessed October 11, 2017, http://www.economist.com/node/1632343.

98. Ibid.

99. Banerjee, "Hybrid Car Technology."

100. Michael Shnayerson, *The Car That Could: The Inside Story of GM's Revolutionary Electric Vehicle* (New York: Random House, 1996), 39.

101. Ibid., 40.

102. Ibid.

# Index

CPSIA information can be obtained
at www.ICGtesting.com
Printed in the USA
LVHW05s1746070618
579966LV00002B/226/P